PEOPLE
IN THE NEWS

Steven Spielberg

by Adam Woog

Lucent Books, San Diego, CA

Titles in the People in the News series include:
Bill Gates
Michael Jordan
The Rolling Stones
Steven Spielberg
Oprah Winfrey

To Harold Elias and Mary Alice Tully,
my favorite movie addicts

Library of Congress Cataloging-in-Publication Data

Woog, Adam, 1953–
   Steven Spielberg / by Adam Woog.
      p. cm. — (People in the news)
   Summary: Explores the public and private lives of Steven
Spielberg, who has combined popular storytelling with artistic
creativity to become hailed as the most successful film director
in the world.
   ISBN 1-56006-361-0 (lib. bdg. : alk. paper)
   1. Spielberg, Steven, 1947–   —Juvenile literature.
2. Motion picture producers and directors—United States—
Biography—Juvenile literature. [1. Spielberg, Steven,
1947–   . 2. Motion picture producers and directors.] I. Title.
II. Series: People in the news (San Diego, Calif.)
PN1998.3.S65W66   1999
791.43'0233'092—dc21
[b]   98-7463
                                                       CIP
                                                       AC

Copyright © 1999 by Lucent Books, Inc.
P.O. Box 289011
San Diego, CA 92198-9011
Printed in the U.S.A.

Table of Contents

Foreword

Fame and celebrity are alluring. People are drawn to those who walk in fame's spotlight, whether they are known for great accomplishments or for notorious deeds. The lives of the famous pique public interest and attract attention, perhaps because their experiences seem in some ways so different from, yet in other ways so similar to, our own.

Newspapers, magazines, and television regularly capitalize on this fascination with celebrity by running profiles of famous people. For example, television programs such as *Entertainment Tonight* devote all of their programming to stories about entertainment and entertainers. Magazines such as *People* fill their pages with stories of the private lives of famous people. Even newspapers, newsmagazines, and television news frequently delve into the lives of well-known personalities. Despite the number of articles and programs, few provide more than a superficial glimpse at their subjects.

Lucent's People in the News series offers young readers a deeper look into the lives of today's newsmakers, the influences that have shaped them, and the impact they have had in their fields of endeavor and on other people's lives. The subjects of the series hail from many disciplines and walks of life. They include authors, musicians, athletes, political leaders, entertainers, entrepreneurs, and others who have made a mark on modern life and who, in many cases, will continue to do so for years to come.

These biographies are more than factual chronicles. Each book emphasizes the contributions, accomplishments, or deeds that have brought fame or notoriety to the individual and shows how that person has influenced modern life. Authors portray their subjects in a realistic, unsentimental light. For example, Bill Gates—the cofounder and chief executive officer of the software giant Microsoft—has been instrumental in making personal computers the most vital tool of the modern age. Few dispute his business savvy, his perseverance, or his technical expertise, yet critics say he is ruthless in his dealings with competitors and driven more by his desire to maintain Microsoft's dominance in the computer industry than by an interest in furthering technology.

In these books, young readers will encounter inspiring stories about real people who achieved success despite enormous obstacles. Oprah Winfrey—the most powerful, most watched, and wealthiest woman on television today—spent the first six years of her life in the care of her grandparents while her unwed mother sought work and a better life elsewhere. Her adolescence was colored by promiscuity, pregnancy at age fourteen, rape, and sexual abuse.

Each author documents and supports his or her work with an array of primary and secondary source quotations taken from diaries, letters, speeches, and interviews. All quotes are footnoted to show readers exactly how and where biographers derive their information and provide guidance for further research. The quotations enliven the text by giving readers eyewitness views of the life and accomplishments of each person covered in the People in the News series.

In addition, each book in the series includes photographs, annotated bibliographies, timelines, and comprehensive indexes. For both the casual reader and the student researcher, the People in the News series offers insight into the lives of today's newsmakers—people who shape the way we live, work, and play in the modern age.

Hollywood Icon

> *By now a billion Earthlings have seen [Spielberg's] films. They have only one thing in common. They have all, at some stage, been children.*
> —writer Martin Amis

> *Most people dream. Steven dreams—then he fulfills.*
> —Leah Spielberg Adler, Steven's mother

STEVEN SPIELBERG IS, by almost any measurement, the most successful filmmaker in the world. Perhaps more than any other director, he has managed the difficult task of combining popular storytelling and artistic creativity with the harsh restrictions of the business world.

As a result, Spielberg has become a Hollywood icon. His movies top the lists of all-time box-office champs. They are works of skill and imagination that, with only a few exceptions, have stood the test of time. Spielberg himself has influenced how the film industry works, and he has inspired a generation of younger directors.

More people have seen, enjoyed, and been moved by Spielberg movies than those of any other director in history. His friend and sometime collaborator George Lucas says that this combination of factors puts Spielberg in a remarkable position:

> People like Steven don't come along every day, and when they do, it's an amazing thing. It's like talking about Einstein or Babe Ruth or Tiger Woods. He's not in a group of film-makers his age; he's far, far away.[1]

Steven Spielberg (far right) at the premier of his film Indiana Jones and the Temple of Doom. *With Spielberg are (left to right) George Lucas, the film's executive producer, and stars Kate Capshaw and Ke Huy Quan.*

Although Spielberg often deals in the realm of the supernatural, the superhero, and fantasy, many claim to see autobiographical elements in his films. He has translated many events in his life directly onto the screen, especially those from his childhood. For instance, the suburban life of *Poltergeist* and *E.T.*, as well as the boy's fascination with flight in *Empire of the Sun*, were all directly inspired by the director's life. Spielberg's mother remarks, "You are viewing our family at the dinner table when you see *E.T.*" [2]

Spielberg's life has been the subject of dozens of interviews, books, and documentaries. Although in many ways very private, he is open about some aspects of his personal life.

For instance, he has talked frankly about the years of unhappiness he endured while his parents were breaking up, and the fact that he has reconciled with his father only recently. The director has also spoken about other personal problems and breakthroughs; for example, what he calls his "delayed adolescence," his ambiguous feelings about his religion, his troubled first marriage and painful divorce, and the stability he has found in recent years as a devoted father and husband.

In addition, Spielberg can be forthcoming about some of his minor foibles and failings, many of them leftovers from his childhood. He admits to having been a lifelong nail-biter, for instance. He avoids elevators and airplanes when possible, and he compulsively sucks on a finger when thinking on the set. Furthermore, he hates disciplining his kids: "I'm the guy who tries to keep the kids downstairs when my wife is trying to get them to bed."[3]

He is also cheerfully candid about his lack of Hollywood glitz. Remarking on his infrequent attendance at parties, the director says, "When I do go, I'm the guy in the corner eating all the dip."[4] And his casual dress style—typically a baseball hat, T-shirt, jeans, and sneakers—has inspired both widespread imitation and widespread mockery. His friend and colleague, actor Tom Hanks, remarks, "Sometimes you want to say, 'Steven, the hat! The hat!' I mean, he's written the book on ball caps."[5]

Block Parties

Spielberg's phenomenal success is due to many factors. One is his ability to maintain close access to the joys and fears of childhood; in many ways, as Spielberg himself cheerfully admits, he is just an overgrown kid. At the same time, he has intense focus. Richard Dreyfuss, the star of *Jaws* and *Close Encounters*, says of his friend,

Steven Spielberg, flanked by his mother, Leah Adler (left), and wife, Kate Capshaw, is shown here at the 1994 Academy Awards.

What comes out of Steven unconsciously is that he's a big
kid who at twelve years old decided to make movies, and
he's still twelve years old—he's focused every one of his
powers and capabilities on making movies and blocked
everything else in the world out of his personality.[6]

Another factor is the director's technical ability, which produces images on the screen that rival any of those created by other
film greats. Spielberg greatly admires directors with sweeping epic
styles and overwhelming visual appeal, such as David Lean and
Stanley Kubrick; his films owe much of their power to his sheer
joy in creating striking visual images. At the same time, he (and his
stable of gifted editors, cinematographers, and writers) are able to
create fast-paced and exciting story lines.

Further enhancing Spielberg's ability is his knack for tap-
ping directly into and thoroughly mining a single emotion. This
reach for "super-intensity," as the director calls it, lets Spielberg
focus relentlessly on a given feeling, such as hatred, anxiety,
love, or devotion. Writer Martin Amis remarks, "His films beam
down on an emotion and then subject it to two hours of muscu-
lar titillation [stimulation]."[7]

*Steven Spielberg has
delighted audiences with
many of the most popular
movies in history and
inspired a new generation
of directors.*

Awful Light

Asked to name the single image that best sums up his filmmaking, Spielberg offered this thought to interviewers Roger Ebert and Gene Siskel, in the book *The Future of the Movies.*

> I think it's the little boy in *Close Encounters* opening the door and standing in that beautiful yet awful light, just like fire coming through the doorway. And he's very small, and it's a very large door, and there's a lot of promise or danger outside that door. . . .
>
> [W]e don't know what's out there, and yet we should discover what's out there. We should be afraid of not knowing. And we should take a step toward what we don't understand and what we don't know about and what scares us. And we should embrace what scares us. We shouldn't be self-destructive about it, but we should go toward that kind of proverbial light and see what's out there for us.

A scene from Close Encounters of the Third Kind.

Another factor is Spielberg's wide range of interests. He admires old-fashioned journeyman filmmakers such as Victor Fleming, who made, among many others, *The Wizard of Oz.* Directors like Fleming were good at adapting themselves to new situations, using a variety of styles quickly and within the confines of the studio system. Like them, Spielberg is able to use his broad interests to create a variety of works on many subjects. Richard Dreyfuss wryly remarks, "Steven could do whole movies about block parties if he wanted to."[8]

"I Am the Audience"

Still another factor in Spielberg's success is his unpretentious style. He avoids making movies that are difficult to understand, with pompous subjects and self-important images. Instead, Spielberg strives to make films that are simple enough for naive viewers to understand, but complex enough to engage more sophisticated audiences.

This unpretentious style can be traced to Spielberg's background, which was, in many ways, quite ordinary. He did not come from wealth or privilege, and he did not get his training at an esoteric film school. He is a product of middle-class American suburbs, and he learned his craft as an apprentice in the workaday television industry. As a result, he can make movies that (with a few exceptions) connect remarkably well with most audiences.

Spielberg has often remarked that the people in his stories are ordinary humans put into extraordinary situations. Audiences find it easy to identify with such everyday heroes. He has also remarked that he makes movies that he wants to see, which are usually the same movies that he thinks most audiences want to see. He elaborates:

> I've often taken the approach . . . that I am the audience. Lucky enough to have been given a camera at an early age and allowed to make movies for myself and, therefore, my friends sitting in the dark. So I've made movies that are bigger than life and movies that haven't happened to me, but stories that I wish would happen to me and characters I wish I could be more like.[9]

Steven Spielberg's own story begins shortly after the end of World War II in a city in the Midwest.

Chapter 1

A Formative Childhood

Steven Allan Spielberg was born on December 18, 1946, at Jewish Hospital in Cincinnati, Ohio, the oldest Jewish hospital in the United States. Steven was the first child of Arnold Spielberg and Leah Posner Spielberg and the first grandchild on either side of the family. (Many sources erroneously list his birthdate as 1947.)

The Spielberg and Posner families had much in common. Both were Jewish. Both were originally from Russia, but both had been part of Cincinnati's large Jewish community since early in the century. The heads of both families were merchants.

Arnold's father Shmuel (later called Samuel) came to America as a young man in 1906. He found work as a peddler and grocer in Cincinnati, and two years after his arrival in America arranged for his wife, Rebecca, to join him. Rebecca became active in local Democratic politics while raising Arnold and two other children, Irvin and Natalie.

Leah's family, the Posners, had a similar story. Her father, Fievel (Philip) Posner, arrived in Cincinnati in 1905 and was a grocer before moving into "jobbing," selling odd lots of merchandise wholesale to storekeepers. This work supported his wife, Jennie, a Cincinnati native, and their children, Leah and Bernard.

Parents

Several important themes in the adult Steven Spielberg's moviemaking can be traced to his parents, who had contrasting interests and personalities.

Serious-minded and rather distant, Arnold Spielberg had always been interested in science. As a boy, he was constantly tinkering with radios or reading science fiction. He served in the China-Burma-India theater during World War II as a radio operator for the U.S. Army Air Force. After the war, Arnold received a degree in electrical engineering and specialized in a then-new field: computer technology. He had been dating Leah Posner since 1939, and he married her in 1945 as the war was winding down.

In contrast to her husband, Leah had a fun-loving sense of humor, a knack for getting along with people, and a quick, bubbly wit. She often joked that her wit made up for a lack of beauty, saying that if she'd had a pug nose she wouldn't have needed to develop a personality.

Leah was a talented classical pianist. She had once hoped for a career as a concert musician, but after graduating from music school she found a job as a social worker. Although she continued to play piano, she never pursued it professionally.

Steven Spielberg inherited creativity from his mother (far left) and an industrious nature from his father (second from left).

Steven apparently inherited some of his temperament and gifts from each of his parents. For example, although he was a poor

student at school, Steven often imitated Arnold's workaholic tendencies when it came to filmmaking, obsessively studying new techniques to maintain an edge in a competitive field. Steven also inherited a creative and dreamy side to his personality from Leah. This led to his love of storytelling and visual spectacle.

Spielberg recalls the contrasts in the household made by his parents' diverging interests and temperaments:

> [My mother] would have chamber concerts in the living room with her friends who played the viola and the violin and the harp. While that was happening, in another room my father would be conferring with nine or ten men about computers [with] graphs and charts and oscilloscopes and transistors.[10]

Culturally Jewish

Steven's parents, like many children of Jewish immigrants, were more culturally Jewish than observant; in other words, they had a strong sense of cultural identity but did not regularly attend synagogue. Also, they practiced dietary and other traditional Jewish laws only intermittently. Nonetheless, Spielberg says that his first memory is of being carried through a synagogue and seeing the faces of elderly, bearded men looking down on him.

Spielberg has also remarked that he learned his first numbers by studying the tattoo on the arm of a man who was taking English lessons from his grandmother Jennie. The tattoo branded the man as a survivor of the concentration camps set up during the war, still a vivid memory in the minds of Jews in the late 1940s. These reminders of Nazi terror would later be crucial to Spielberg the filmmaker.

Leaving Family Behind

Steven loved to visit his grandfather Fievel's house, which was always stocked with *shmatte*—a Yiddish word meaning clothing and accessories. Fievel's house had an ever-changing array of socks, shoelaces, bow ties, and other *shmatte* that Steven's grandfather sold to stores. Such an inventory was great fun for a child with an active imagination.

Fievel, who loved to dance and sing, and his brother, Steven's Uncle Boris, fed the boy's creative side. Boris was the first person in the family to enter show business. He was a Shakespearean actor on the then-thriving Yiddish-language theater circuit and later became a lion tamer in a circus.

Steven loved to hear stories about his far-off but exciting and exotic Uncle Boris. The filmmaker later honored his grandfather by naming the main character in *An American Tail* after him and incorporating some of his stories about Russia into it.

When Steven was only two, the Spielbergs left the grandparents and the close-knit community they knew in Cincinnati. From then on, the Spielbergs would live in a series of bland suburban settings, with a constantly changing set of acquaintances and neighbors. Only occasionally would family visits bring Steven back in contact with his Cincinnati friends and relatives.

In 1949 the family moved to New Jersey, living first in Camden and then nearby Haddon Township. Arnold had been offered a job working for RCA on their early computer systems. Steven's three sisters were born during the family's stay in New Jersey: Anne in 1949, Susan in 1953, and Nancy in 1956.

A Terror to His Sisters

As he grew, Steven's personality became more defined. He had always been bright and curious; his family joked that his first word was "why?" He also had an especially strong visual sense, seeing the world in new and different ways or imagining new and highly visual scenarios.

However, he was an indifferent student who consistently earned Cs through elementary school. Arnold was always nagging his son to study harder, with little success. Leah, on the other hand, was tolerant of Steven's mediocre studies and sometimes eccentric behavior.

For example, she let him keep a number of parakeets flying freely around his room. His room was such a mess that Leah would not even enter it; the most she did was to open the door to grope for his laundry bag.

A nonstop terror to his sisters and other kids, Steven constantly teased them with spooky stories and weird games. He could be so

mean that some babysitters in the neighborhood said they would take care of Steven's sisters only if he wasn't there.

Sometimes he would scare

As a child, Steven terrorized his sisters (left to right) Nancy, Susan (behind their mother, Leah), and Anne with scary pranks.

his little sisters by hiding outside their rooms and eerily howling, "I am the moon!" Once, he cut off the head of his sister's favorite doll and served it to her on a plate surrounded with tomatoes and lettuce. "If I had known any better," Steven's mother remarks, "I would have taken him to a psychiatrist, and then there would have been no *E. T.* His badness was so original that there weren't even books to tell you what to do."[11]

Scary Scenes

On another occasion he rigged up an elaborate and scary scene in a bedroom closet. It was organized around a plastic skull lit from inside by a light bulb. Steven carefully created a display with the skull and some World War II–vintage military clothing his father had saved.

He convinced his sisters that a mummified soldier was in the closet, then somehow persuaded them to enter it. As the door closed, he turned on the light in the skull—with terrifying results.

Spielberg has often remarked that such tricks were, at least in part, a reflection of his own fears. He feared many things as a boy, including tree shadows and monsters that hid under his bed or in the cracks of his bedroom walls. A television documentary about snakes terrified him so much that he cried for days.

Many of these fears would later reappear in Spielberg films, such as the menacing shadow tree and clown doll in *Poltergeist* and Indiana Jones's fear of snakes.

The First Movie

In 1952, Steven saw his first movie. His father took him to *The Greatest Show on Earth*, a film made late in the career of the pioneering director Cecil B. De Mille.

Arnold had told his son that they were going to "a circus movie." The boy heard the word "circus" and so was expecting the real thing, which he was familiar with; he was initially let down when he saw only a two-dimensional flat screen. Soon, though, he was amazed as the characters on the flat screen seemed to come to life. He recalls:

Many of the frightening scenes from Spielberg's movies stem from his own childhood fears. Here, ghosts attempt to capture a child in Poltergeist.

"What's Happening Here?"

This memory, excerpted from John Baxter's *Steven Spielberg: The Unauthorized Biography*, is of an important moment in young Spielberg's life—watching a meteor shower in the desert.

My dad woke me in the middle of the night and rushed me into our car in my night clothes. I didn't know what was happening. It was frightening. My mom wasn't with me. So I thought, "What's happening here?" He had a thermos of coffee and had brought blankets and we drove for about half an hour. We finally pulled over to the side of the road, and there were a couple of hundred people, lying on their backs in the middle of the night, looking up at the sky. My dad found a place, and we both lay down. He pointed to the sky, and there was a magnificent meteor shower. All these incredible points of light were criss-crossing the sky. It was a phenomenal display, apparently announced in advance by the weather bureau.

My father said: "It's going to be bigger than you, but that's all right. The people in it are going to be up on a screen and they can't get out at you." But there they were up on that screen and they were getting out at me. I guess ever since then I've wanted to try to involve the audience as much as I can, so they no longer think they're sitting in an audience.[12]

More Influences

For years, Steven's film experiences were relatively bland. He was allowed to go to the movies only with his parents; what he saw was suitable for both adults and kids, such as light comedies, musicals, and Disney shows.

But Steven's fertile visual imagination was fed in other ways as well. Steven loved comic books, especially Superman, Batman, Donald Duck, and the irreverent *Mad* magazine. There were puppet shows that he staged for the neighbors. And there was, of course, television.

Steven's was the first generation to grow up with TV as an everyday part of life, and he embraced it wholeheartedly: Westerns, situation comedies, police shows, and, perhaps most of all, Disney's Sunday night specials. "Walt Disney was my parental conscience," he remarks, "and my step-parent was the TV set."[13]

Steven's parents tried restricting his TV time. They draped the set with a cover to make it less conspicuous. For a time, Arnold would lay a strategically placed hair across the controls in an attempt to tell when Steven had been watching it without permission. Steven recalls, "I always found the hair, memorized its position, and replaced it when I was through."[14]

Another Move

Early in 1957, when Steven was ten, the family moved again. Leaving behind a familiar environment to go someplace new is a theme from Spielberg's childhood that recurs in his later movies. He says:

> Just as I'd become accustomed to a school and a teacher and a best friend, the FOR SALE sign would dig into the front lawn. . . . And it would always be that inevitable good-bye scene, in the train station or at the carport packing up the car to drive somewhere, or at the airport. Where all my friends would be there and we'd say good-bye to each other and I would leave.[15]

This time, Arnold had been offered a job in Arizona with General Electric. In the Southwest, Steven would attend junior and senior high—and he would begin making movies.

Chapter 2

Early Films, Early Themes

My growing up was like a sitcom ABC buys for a season before they drop it.

—Steven Spielberg

THE SPIELBERGS SETTLED in Scottsdale, a suburb of Phoenix, Arizona. Steven had never felt very much at home in New Jersey, and in many ways the Southwest was an even stranger environment.

Scottsdale itself was made up primarily of new suburbs that had once been citrus groves. It was hot and dry and full of strange new sights to the young boy, such as men driving pickup trucks and wearing string ties and cowboy boots. Surrounding the town was desert, which to Steven was a scary place full of gila monsters, odd plants, and big insects.

When Steven started attending Ingleside Elementary School, his slender build, unathletic ways, and strange accent did not let him fit in easily. He was shy and withdrawn throughout his grade school years. Eleanor Wolf, his sixth-grade teacher, recalls,

> I felt sorry for him because he didn't have any friends. You see, he was different from everybody else. . . . He was rather nondescript, just a good little kid. . . . Oh, heavens, never in my wildest dreams did I imagine Steven Spielberg would have grown up to be anything like he is.[16]

Meteors

Arnold Spielberg liked the desert environment around his new home, and often took his family on expeditions. One such event later was transformed into a famous scene in a Spielberg movie: the episode in *Close Encounters* when a group of people gathers to witness a flyby of UFOs at night.

On this occasion, Arnold woke Steven in the middle of the night, bundled the sleepy boy into the car, and drove out into the desert. According to Steven, they stopped in an area where hundreds of others were gathered, though according to Arnold they were alone. In either case, they were there to watch a spectacular meteor shower. Steven recalls:

> My father was a computer scientist. He gave me a technical explanation of what was happening. "These meteors are space debris attracted by the gravitational . . ." But I didn't want to hear that. I wanted to think of them as falling stars.[17]

Witnessing the meteors with his father was an important moment for Steven. It represented the balance of science: the wonder and spiritual mystery of the cosmos on the one hand and

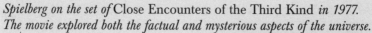

Spielberg on the set of Close Encounters of the Third Kind *in 1977. The movie explored both the factual and mysterious aspects of the universe.*

hard-science, rational technology on the other. This balance would later become a theme he explored again and again in his own art.

Home Movies

Steven's first films, made before he was even a teenager, were home movies. He shot them with a twenty-dollar, 8-millimeter camera that Leah had given Arnold.

At first Arnold took the family's home movies. Steven was not shy about criticizing his father's technique, however, constantly suggesting different camera angles and lighting strategies. Eventually, Arnold simply handed the camera to his son and told him to take over.

Steven discovered that he liked taking records of his family's camping trips and other adventures. More than that, he liked staging the events he was shooting to create maximum storytelling effect. Before long, he was turning even the simplest events into epic sagas.

A simple shot of the family car leaving a camping spot, for instance, would start with an extreme close-up of a car tire, then gradually zoom backwards to show the whole car rolling away. Soon, Steven was insisting that even simple events had to be carefully staged: "My dad had to wait for me to say 'Action!' before he could put the knife in the fish to clean it," Spielberg recalls. Joking about the violence involved in slicing open a fish, he adds, "That was my first PG-13 moment."[18]

First Movies

Steven's casual creation of home movies soon blossomed into a major hobby, and from there into an all-consuming passion. He recalls,

> I was more or less a boy with a passion for a hobby that grew out of control and somewhat consumed me. . . . I knew after my third or fourth little 8mm epic that this was going to be a career, not just a hobby.[19]

Steven's first "epic"—not just a home movie documenting a family outing—involved toy trains that he set up to crash into each other. Even at this early stage he was experimenting with unusual camera angles; this film included cutaway shots showing tiny plastic men recoiling in horror from the collision.

The first Spielberg movie with a narrative story was made in 1958 to earn a photography merit badge in Steven's Boy Scout troop. This movie (which has not survived) was a brief Western variously called *The Last Gunfight, The Last Shootout,* and *The Last Gun.* In a joking reference to the TV show *Gunsmoke,* Steven sometimes called it *Gunsmog.* Steven's friends starred, dressed up as cowboys and bandits. The main set was a replica of a Western stagecoach that stood in front of a local steak house.

Growing Obsession

Steven followed up with increasingly sophisticated and varied stories. In the eighth grade alone, for instance, he made a couple of comedies, a mystery, and *Fighter Squad,* the first in what would become a recurring theme: epics involving World War II and Nazis.

Fighter Squad was a fifteen-minute black-and-white movie. It was shot at a local air force base using vintage aircraft and authentic props that were souvenirs from Arnold's Army Air Corps days. It also used "real" movie techniques such as shooting in front of painted backdrops and using electric fans to make the hair of the pilots blow realistically in the wind.

As Steven spent more and more of his allowance and free time making movies, his father became increasingly skeptical about the new obsession. However, Leah was more of a willing partner.

She often let Steven stay home from school so he could edit his films. As his productions grew more elaborate, she also let him virtually take over the house. She recalls that the family living room had essentially no furniture, except for her piano, so that Steven could mount various scenes there and have room for lighting equipment.

On one occasion, she let him blow up a pressure cooker full of cherries so that he could get the fake blood and gore he needed. She claimed that she was still finding bits of the mess to clean up years later.

She liked the fact that his involvement with movies let her keep tabs on his whereabouts. "We're all for Steven's hobby," she remarked at the time. "This way we know and the parents of his teenage friends know where they are; they're not cruising up and down Central Avenue."[20]

Watching Movies

As Steven's interest in creating movies grew, so did his interest in watching them. He grew up with a steady diet of movies, both disposable junk and the classics. This was the beginning of his lifelong, self-taught education in film scholarship.

For Steven, the best place for seeing movies was the Kiva Theater in Scottsdale. The Saturday kids' matinee there was a bargain: for fifty cents, Steven and his friends could see two features plus ten cartoons and shorts. Sometimes the selections would include old-fashioned cliffhanger serials like the ones Steven and George Lucas would later pay tribute to with the Indiana Jones series.

As an adolescent, Steven saw many movies that would directly affect his own later work. Among these were David Lean's classic epics *Bridge over the River Kwai* and *Lawrence of Arabia.* Spielberg has often cited Lean's sweeping narrative sense and visual style as his greatest influences. After seeing *Lawrence* in 1962, Spielberg recalls, he "really kicked into high gear and thought, 'This I gotta do. I gotta make movies.'"[21]

Leah Adler has supported her son Steven's moviemaking since he was a teenager, even letting him stay home from school to work on his films.

Feeding the Obsession

Steven's interest in viewing other people's movies was not satisfied by seeing them in theaters. He began showing films in his living room. He periodically rented 16-millimeter prints of movies, such as classic comedies by Charlie Chaplin and the Marx Brothers, and showed them to a paying audience of friends and neighbors. His sisters sold concessions and took tickets, and Steven used his own short films as curtain raisers.

Soundtracks comprised another aspect of Steven's interest. He already played the clarinet in the school band, inspired by his mother's love for music, and he expanded that interest to include movie music.

Steven quickly realized that soundtracks can have a powerful effect on the suspense level and emotional impact of a film. He started collecting recordings of movie soundtracks. He built some of his films around portions of these classic soundtracks. As his equipment became sophisticated enough to include sound recording, he also composed brief segments of original music to accompany some of his movies.

In later years, John Williams's scores for Spielberg films like *Jaws* and *Raiders of the Lost Ark* would be some of the most memorable movie soundtracks ever recorded. Steven's collecting hobby, meanwhile, continued into adulthood; today he owns hundreds of rare soundtrack recordings and reportedly can sing long stretches of them from memory.

Not Worth a Dime

In this reminiscence from Joseph McBride's *Steven Spielberg: A Biography*, Spielberg's mother Leah recalls their chaotic household-turned-film studio.

Our house was run like a studio. We really worked hard for him. Your life was not worth a dime if you didn't, because he nagged you like crazy. Steven had this way of directing everything. Not just his movies, his life. He directed our household. . . .

He was a terrible student in school. But I never thought, What's going to become of him? Maybe if it had crossed my mind, I'd have gotten worried.

The soundtrack of Spielberg's movie Jaws *is one of the most famous musical scores ever recorded. Even before his success with* Jaws, *Steven understood the importance of music in movies.*

In 1961, Steven started his freshman year at Arcadia High School in Phoenix. In a school where athletic ability was important and students with intellectual interests like film did not fit in, the unathletic and generally unsociable Steven was definitely an odd man out. "I was the weird, skinny kid with the acne," he recalls. "I was a wimp."[22]

Nonetheless, he discovered that filmmaking was a way for him to make friends. His encyclopedic knowledge of movies attracted a small circle of like-minded kids. Even outside this group, plenty of other kids eagerly lined up to perform in his movies and couldn't wait to see themselves on screen. Steven recalls, "I discovered something I could do, and people would be interested in it and me."[23]

Steven dated only very casually in high school. Perhaps he felt that his money and time were better spent on movies. Perhaps it was his skinniness and embarassment over his appearance. He was so ashamed of his prominent nose, for instance, that at one point he tried to make it tilt up by putting one end of a piece of duct tape on his forehead and the other on the tip of his nose.

According to his sister Anne, however, Steven was attractive to many girls, especially because of the enthusiasm he displayed about his hobby. She recalls:

> Some of my friends had major crushes on him. If you looked at a picture of him then, you'd say, Yes, there's a nerd. . . . But he really had an incredible personality. He could make people do things. He made everything he was going to do sound like you wished you were a part of it.[24]

"Film Was Power"

On one occasion in high school, Steven used filmmaking to defuse a potentially difficult situation involving a religious bully.

Steven was occasionally harassed by anti-Semitics, people who are prejudiced against Jews. One such bully began tormenting Steven as he was preparing to make his first long film, *Escape to Nowhere.*

Still Childlike

Spielberg's high school friend, Rick Cook, has this to say about the environment they shared in the early 1960s. Cook's observation is reprinted in Joseph McBride's *Steven Spielberg: A Biography.*

One of the interesting things about that milieu is that it was so new, everybody was from somewhere else, and a lot of the old ethnic associations didn't exist. Looking back, there were a fair number of Jews at the school—who knew? Who cared?. . .

By the time I knew "Spielbug," he knew what he was going to do. But he was not narcissistic about it. The thing with him was not ego, not the shallow sense of "I'm going to be a big movie director." What interested him was making the movie, the whole process. He is still childlike in the sense that he is still fascinated with magic and a sense of wonder, but he was one of the least childish fourteen-year-olds I had ever seen. He was very focused and that's not a fourteen-year-old's characteristic. If anyone I knew was going to make it, I thought he was going to, because he was so driven and committed.

Steven chose to counterattack. He boldly asked the bully to play an important role in the film. The bully surprised Steven by accepting, and the two gradually came to accept each other more. The experience taught Steven important lessons in the capacity for film to bring wildly different people together, and in his own ability to control situations through moviemaking. "I had learned," Steven later commented, "that film was power."[25]

Escape to Nowhere

Escape to Nowhere was a forty-minute, silent, color World War II saga. With this film, Steven again used his knack for assembling professional-looking props. In this case, he was able to borrow a pickup truck carrying an army surplus 50-caliber machine gun. Leah or Arnold did the driving; they were the only ones on the crew with licenses.

The Spielberg talent for innovation was taking shape even at this early stage. For instance, Steven recruited twenty or thirty kids to play extras, but he didn't have enough Nazi helmets. He told the helmeted extras to run in front of the camera, then double around in back of the camera and hand the helmets off to other kids. These new kids then took their own turns. On camera, it looked as though a continuous stream of soldiers was running past.

Steven also invented clever ways to create special effects. He discovered that flour, kicked up when an actor stepped on a fulcrumed plank, was an excellent simulated bomb detonation. He used miniatures, too; on one occasion he cut doors and windows in a cardboard box and set it on fire to create a burning building.

Escape to Nowhere's high production values and innovative style won Steven first prize in a statewide amateur filmmaking contest. The prizes included a good camera and a library of books about moviemaking. To go with his new treasures, Steven's father bought him a good-quality projector and a sound system so he could record dialogue and music on film.

Firelight

Using the new equipment, Steven was able to produce his first feature-length film. This was a science-fiction epic called *Firelight*, the young director's most ambitious undertaking yet.

Copies of *Firelight* apparently still exist, but Spielberg has never made them public and has often dismissed the movie to reporters as "terrible." The story is about an obsessed UFO expert who is tracking an extraterrestrial that kidnaps a dog and a girl, played by Steven's sister Nancy. *Firelight* apparently mirrors a later movie, *Close Encounters*, not only in this basic storyline but also in many specific scenes.

As always, Steven was the primary force behind the production, but he also had some help. The Arcadia High School band recorded the musical score, which Steven wrote. Arnold persuaded some General Electric engineer friends to help with the sound synchronization, which matches up the soundtrack to the visual images.

Steven was reportedly calm and organized on the set, with no harsh words for his hardworking cast and crew. This trait has carried into Spielberg's adult life, and he has a reputation for generally being friendly, relaxed, and gentle on the set. Because of his ability to manipulate complex scenes and large groups during the filming of *Firelight,* his mother called him "Cecil B. DeSpielberg"—a joking but proud reference to the pioneer director Cecil B. De Mille.

The extraterrestrial visitors and story line of Close Encounters of the Third Kind *(pictured) were based on* Firelight, *a movie Spielberg created in 1964.*

Firelight premiered early in 1964 at the Kiva Theater, which Steven rented out for the occasion. A limousine was provided for the director and stars, driven by the father of a cast member; a floodlight was donated by a local shopping center to provide added glamour to the opening. Steven sold out the theater and made a modest profit over the $600 it had cost to film his epic.

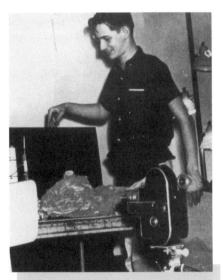

This photo shows a teenage Steven Spielberg creating a set for his first full-length feature, the science-fiction movie Firelight.

California Troubles

The day after the premiere, the Spielberg family moved again. Once more, the move was prompted by the offer of a new job for Arnold, and it meant another suburban community, another new school, another new set of friends. This time the Spielbergs headed to the small town of Saratoga, in what would eventually become Silicon Valley near San Jose, California.

Spielberg has often remarked that his final two years of high school in California were "hell on earth" because they marked his first serious encounters with anti-Semitism.

The athletes and surfers who dominated the social life at Saratoga High tormented Steven by calling him names, striking him when they passed in the halls, and throwing pennies—a cruel taunt reflecting the prejudice that Jews have an abnormally strong interest in money. For a time, Steven had to be picked up at school by his mother because he was afraid to walk home by himself.

However, other Jewish students who attended Saratoga High at the time have disputed the fierceness of Steven's memory, saying that it was never as bad as he recalls. Steven's best friend in those years, who was Lutheran, says that he never saw anything overtly anti-Semitic. Perhaps, some biographers have suggested, this disparity was an example of Spielberg's imagination inflating an episode to larger-than-life size, as would often happen in films later.

End of a Marriage

Except for a few shorts, Steven made no movies during this period. Although he applied himself to his studies, and his grades improved from his usual Ds to Cs and Bs, he spent much of the time in a mildly depressed mood. Some observers suggest that this stemmed from his unhappiness at home.

For years, Leah and Arnold had been unhappy together. Most of the time, this unease made itself known simply as a feeling around the house, though it did sometimes degenerate into loud arguments. Steven recalls of his parents, "I don't think they were aware of how acutely *we* were aware of their unhappiness— not violence, just a pervading unhappiness you could cut with a fork or a spoon at dinner every night." [26]

Things finally reached a low point, and Arnold moved out. He relocated in Los Angeles around the time Steven graduated from Saratoga High. Leah filed for divorce the following year.

When Steven went to spend the summer after graduation with his father, it marked the end of one period in his life and the beginning of a new one: his apprenticeship in professional filmmaking.

Chapter 3

Self-Education and Professional Breakthroughs

The director of that movie is the greatest young talent to come along in years.
—legendary director Billy Wilder
after seeing a preview of Spielberg's first
theatrical feature, *The Sugarland Express*

STEVEN FINISHED HIGH SCHOOL with a C average, not good enough to get him into a university with a film department such as the University of Southern California (USC) or the University of California at Los Angeles (UCLA).

Instead, he enrolled as an English major at California State University at Long Beach in 1967. He could have chosen not to go to college at all. One reason to go, however, was that as a student he could avoid the draft for the Vietnam War. Another was to satisfy his father's desire to see him pursue a higher education.

He chose Long Beach because it was close to Hollywood. He stayed with his father in the Los Angeles neighborhood of Brentwood and commuted to classes in a '62 Pontiac convertible that Arnold had given him for graduation.

The proximity to Hollywood was perfect for the education Steven had in mind for himself: a relentless self-taught curriculum in films. As compensation for not attending film school, according to journalists Michael Pye and Lynda Myles, he "immersed himself in movie lore":

He watched every film on late night television, memo-
rizing names and faces, recalling shots or credits at will.
He became a scholar of film [and] a graduate of the
school of Hollywood.[27]

Universal Knowledge

A legend persists that as a student Steven bluffed his way onto
the Universal Studios lot every day for three months by wearing a business suit and acting like he belonged there. According
to this story, he found an empty office and put his name on the
door. This story is probably not true.

It is true, however, that he did get a nonpaying job at Universal Studios during the summer before his senior year of high
school. Chuck Silvers, an executive in Universal's editing
department, met with Steven as a favor to a mutual friend of his
and the Spielbergs. Silvers gave him a tour and arranged for
Steven to have access to the studio.

That summer, Steven worked as a clerical assistant in the
editing department. It paid nothing, and most of his actual
duties consisted of mundane work such as running errands to
the developing lab. However, it gave him the opportunity to
roam the Universal lot. He observed TV shows and movies
under production, and he met a variety of people from executives to secretaries.

He discovered that many professionals were happy to share
their knowledge with a bright, inquisitive teenager. For instance,
he learned about editing by watching veterans cut *Wagon Train*
and other television shows.

He also met many legends, including actors Charlton Hes-
ton, Cary Grant, and Rock Hudson; and directors William
Wyler, Franklin Schaffner, and John Cassavetes. Sometimes
Steven, overcoming his shyness, invited celebrities to lunch,
and surprisingly often they accepted. Then he was relentless
about picking their brains.

According to Steven, one day he snuck his way onto a
closed set where one of his great idols, Alfred Hitchcock, was
shooting *Torn Curtain*. Steven says that he was discovered and

kicked off the set. He wryly recalls, "I was bounced by the best."[28]

Informal Apprenticeship

Steven continued this informal apprenticeship as he attended college. Silvers arranged for Steven to be on the Universal lot a few days a week. This helped Steven continue his own tutorial in filmmaking. It was an unusual education, but it was complete; it covered all aspects of the industry, from fine points of technique to obscure aspects of marketing.

In many ways, this was a more useful education than Steven could have found at film school. By observing professionals at work, he learned everyday nuts and bolts instead of abstract theory. This basic education later set him apart from other major directors of his generation, film school graduates such as Martin Scorsese, Francis Coppola, George Lucas, and Brian de Palma.

Unlike his friend George Lucas (left), Steven Spielberg did not study filmmaking at school; his education was an informal apprenticeship at Universal Studios.

Unfortunately, Steven's official studies suffered. He more or less ignored classes unrelated to movies; those that did relate to movies were too basic. Long Beach did not have a formal film program, but it did have a department of radio and television designed to train students for workmanlike jobs such as television camera operators.

It quickly became apparent that Steven was already far beyond anything this program could provide. Hugh Morehead, then chairman of the department, comments:

> I didn't think any of us could teach him anything. Steve knew more about cameras than anybody in the department. He could teach the department. . . . I felt he was passing through on the way to Hollywood.[29]

Steven's relationship with his father grew more bitter over his indifference toward academics and his determination to make movies. Steven eventually moved out of Arnold's apartment and rented a house in West Los Angeles with another Cal State student.

Feeding the Habit

In contrast to many loose, hippie students at the time, Steven was quite straitlaced; he grew his hair fashionably long but never used drugs or cigarettes, rarely drank, and almost never dated. When not studying or making his own films, he spent his time in theaters. Since his father would no longer support his filmmaking expenses, Steven also found odd jobs, such as working in a cafeteria.

He repeatedly tried to interest Universal executives in his work, but they were not willing to look at 8-millimeter film. They said that they would be interested only if he could show them something in 16-millimeter. This was an expensive, complicated process, and he had difficulty completing 16-millimeter projects.

During this period, Steven met Allen Daviau, a promising young cinematographer, who would later be the cinematographer for *E.T.* and other major Spielberg movies. Around the same time, Steven met another future collaborator at a showing of student films: George Lucas, then attending USC.

Amblin'

Early in 1968, Steven met aspiring producer Denis Hoffman. Hoffman put up the twenty thousand dollars Steven needed to shoot his first 16-millimeter film. Shot in the summer of 1968, *Amblin'* was a twenty-minute, wordless romance about a couple hitchhiking to the coast.

The film was edited in six weeks of nonstop activity that fall. The director optimistically wanted to have it ready by the end of the year, so that it could be considered for an Oscar in the live-action short subject category.

Steven has since ridiculed *Amblin'* as "a Pepsi commercial" without soul or content. He consciously made it into a slick piece of work. But it was also strong and assured, and it did what it was supposed to do: It impressed several important Universal executives. In particular, Chuck Silvers thought it was terrific.

In the fall of 1968, Silvers arranged a screening of *Amblin'* for a powerful industry executive: Sidney Sheinberg, Universal Television's vice president for production.

Sheinberg was also impressed with *Amblin'*. "I liked the way he selected the performers, the relationships, the maturity and the warmth that was in that short," the executive recalls. "I told Chuck to have the guy come see me."[30]

Which Would You Rather Do?

Sheinberg had courtly manners and called everyone "sir" or "madam." At that first meeting, he praised a nervous Steven and offered him a job directing for television: "Sir, I liked your film. How would you like to go to work professionally?"[31]

Sheinberg proposed Universal's standard offer for new recruits: a seven-year contract,

Sidney Sheinberg, vice president of production at Universal Television in 1968, offered Spielberg a job after seeing Amblin'.

Lucking Out

Frank Sanello's *Spielberg: The Man, the Movies, the Mythology* contains this passage from a Spielberg interview made shortly after his first big success with *Jaws*.

> I don't think I'm a phenomenon at all, I think part of my success...has to do with lucking out! I think a lot of it has to do with being prepared when the man with the money comes to you and says, "What have you got?" And you fast draw two scripts and three ideas. To go back to the Boy Scouts, the motto was, "Be prepared." And when the time came, I had fifteen films under my right arm. I had three scripts under my left arm, and I was knocking down doors. It was something I wanted to happen, not when I was thirty or thirty-five years old, when most directors start working, but now. By the age of eighteen I was determined to become a professional movie director.

starting at the then-substantial amount of $275 per week. This was the break Steven had been waiting for. Still, he hesitated; he hadn't graduated yet, and he was wary of disappointing his father.

Sheinberg asked the young man which he would rather do: graduate from college or become a director? Put that way, Steven knew the answer was clear. He has often told reporters that he quit college so fast that he didn't even stop to clean out his locker.

One of Steven's first assignments as a salaried Universal employee was to escort a tall young man on a tour around the studio. This was Michael Crichton, a physician-turned-writer who had just sold his novel *The Andromeda Strain* to Universal. The paths of the two men would cross again later, with spectacular results, when they created *Jurassic Park* and *The Lost World*.

"Eyes"

In January 1969, Spielberg began his first directing assignment for the studio: "Eyes," an episode of *Night Gallery*, a series of eerie stories created by Rod Serling, the gifted mastermind behind *The Twilight Zone*.

"Eyes" told the story of a wealthy blind woman who buys a pair of eyes from a desperate gambler and has them implanted in herself. However, when she awakens from surgery her city is experiencing an electrical blackout. Thinking the operation was a failure, she stumbles around her high-rise apartment and crashes through a window.

The story's star was the legendary Joan Crawford. Crawford, then sixty-two, had been in movies since her teens; even though television was a comedown for the celebrated actress, she was still a formidable force. Using a baseball analogy, Spielberg recalls, "Directing Joan Crawford was like pitching to Hank Aaron your first time in the game."[32]

According to Rod Serling's widow Carol, Crawford was skeptical of being directed by someone so young and inexperienced: "Joan was climbing the walls while they were filming. She was calling Rod all the time, and he reassured

Spielberg's early work at Universal included giving a tour of the studios to writer Michael Crichton (top) and directing actress Joan Crawford on the set of "Eyes" (bottom).

Always in Control

In this passage reprinted in Joseph McBride's *Steven Spielberg: A Biography*, the director recalls how he completely missed the social and political experimentation of the 1960s.

I grew up in the sixties, but I was never into flower power, or Vietnam protests, like all my friends. I was always at the movies. . . . I was never part of the drug culture. I never took LSD, mescaline, coke, or anything like that. In my entire life I've probably smoked three joints. But I went through the entire drug period. Several of my friends were heavily into it. I would sit in a room and watch TV while people climbed the walls. I've always been afraid of taking drugs. I've always been afraid of losing control of myself.

her."[33] Still, in person Crawford was gracious to Spielberg, behaving (at least to his face) as though he were a seasoned director. "She treated me like I knew what I was doing, and I didn't," Spielberg says. "I loved her for that."[34]

Perfectionism

For his part, Spielberg did his best to please Crawford. For instance, he knew that she was the widow of the head of Pepsi, and was still on the company's board of directors. So he charmed her by bringing her a single rose each day in a Pepsi bottle.

This is an example of Spielberg's instinct for connecting with others, even those with the stereotypical large egos associated with show business. William Link, the writer who co-created *Columbo*, another show Spielberg worked on early in his career, remarks, "Even then we knew we would all be working for him one day. He was a great politician."[35]

The production speed and values of television are much faster and cheaper than those of film. A typical episode is shot and edited in days, as opposed to weeks or months for a movie. Shooting on "Eyes" went slowly, however, partly because of Spielberg's perfectionism; he wanted to achieve a movielike level of quality and spent long hours setting up elaborate shots. He was humiliated when another director was called in to edit out many of his carefully prepared takes.

Although "Eyes" received good reviews following its broadcast, Spielberg was disappointed with the experience. He was not sure he wanted to continue directing television; he was afraid he could not maintain its demanding pace. He thought about quitting Universal altogether. Wisely, Sheinberg offered an alternative: a paid leave of absence, which Spielberg took from the summer of 1969 through early 1970.

Back on the Job

He used his time off to develop several scripts. One was for a movie about barnstorming pilots of the 1920s, *Ace Eli and Rodger of the Sky*. The movie was eventually made, but it is undistinguished except for the fact that it is the first Hollywood feature to bear Spielberg's name; he receives credit for the story.

In 1970, although he was normally frugal with personal expenses, Spielberg upgraded his living style. He bought a Mercedes convertible and a small house in Laurel Canyon. It was a typically sloppy, casual bachelor pad, its walls covered with movie posters. His only housemate was a cocker spaniel named Elmer.

When he returned to Universal, Spielberg directed several more television shows. As on "Eyes," his crew, mostly seasoned professionals, were at times openly contemptuous of Spielberg's inexperience and time-consuming perfectionism. At one point, the cinematographer for a Spielberg-directed episode of *Columbo* taunted the director by peppering the rest of the crew with sarcastic questions: Does the kid get a milk and cookies break? Will the diaper truck interfere with my generator?

However, with each assignment the young director's talent was more evident, and his crews gradually became more respectful. His reputation within the industry also improved.

Duel

In 1970, Spielberg was offered the chance to write and direct his first feature, a made-for-TV movie called *Duel*. Based on a short story by veteran writer Richard Matheson, the movie was made on a schedule fast even by television standards: sixteen days of shooting and thirteen days of editing.

The result was far superior to most TV movies of the era. It tells the story of David Mann, played by Dennis Weaver, an ordinary salesman who is mysteriously terrorized by a monstrous, smoke-belching truck while driving on a remote mountain road.

There is almost no dialogue, and the viewer never sees the truck driver except for glimpses of an arm and a boot. In the classic style perfected by one of Spielberg's idols, Alfred Hitchcock, the movie is scary because of what is *not* shown. Film critics Donald R. Mott and Cheryl McAllister Saunders note, "Since the driver of the truck is kept from sight, Spielberg lets us fantasize about the possibility that there is no driver at all."[36]

Duel's underlying themes concern losing and regaining control, and how an ordinary person finds the strength to survive an attack by mindless evil. Spielberg comments,

The hero of *Duel* is typical of that lower middle-class American who's been insulated by suburban modernization. A man like that never expects to be challenged by anything more than his television set breaking down and having to call the repairman.[37]

Actor Dennis Weaver portrays a salesman who is attacked by an eerie, fiendish truck in Duel, *Spielberg's first full-length TV movie.*

The movie premiered in November 1971. It was a rousing success with the public, critics, and the industry. *Duel* did so well, in fact, that it was released as a theatrical feature in Europe, Australia, and Japan.

In the week following the broadcast, Spielberg received about a dozen offers to direct feature films. The first two projects he accepted were forgettable TV films, done out of loyalty to Sheinberg: *Something Evil,* about a spirit possessing the son of a couple who have moved to a farmhouse, and *Savage,* about a crusading political journalist.

The Sugarland Express

Spielberg was offered several projects for his first theatrical release, but he held out until he found something in which he could put his own personality. "I didn't want to start my career as a . . . journeyman director," he recalls. "I wanted to do something a little more personal." [38]

In the spring of 1972, Spielberg got the go-ahead for a project he had developed with two writers, Hal Barwood and Matthew Robbins, and a promising new production team, David Brown and Richard Zanuck. *The Sugarland Express* was a comedy/drama based on a real-life incident from 1969. A convict desperate to see his kids breaks out of jail and leads the police on a chase across several states. Along the way, he becomes a kind of folk hero to people in the countryside, who cheer him as he passes.

As reworked by Spielberg and his colleagues, the story's central character became the convict's wife, who convinces her husband to break out of prison and retrieve their child from a foster home. In the key role of Lou Jean, the wife, Spielberg cast Goldie Hawn, then best known as a scatterbrained comic on the TV show *Laugh-In.*

As the story progresses, Lou Jean's desperate chase with her husband turns into a media event, letting Spielberg make a statement about the nature of fame and celebrity. Michael Pye and Lynda Myles comment, "As in *Duel,* [Spielberg's] characters are ordinary folks put into extraordinary situations—Lou Jean and Clovis are small-time casualties of American society, but they become celebrities." [39]

Shooting *Sugarland*

Sugarland was shot early in 1973 near San Antonio, Texas. According to those on the set, Spielberg was in command from the first day of shooting. Unlike many new directors, who are overly timid because they're afraid they'll never get another chance, Spielberg jumped in with confidence. Producer Zanuck remarks,

> I had been around long enough with a lot of great directors [to know] almost immediately that he had knowledge and command and ability, and an innate, intimate sense of the visual mechanics of how you put all those pieces together so that the final result is very striking.[40]

Perhaps because of Spielberg's confidence, the set was more lighthearted than usual. According to Goldie Hawn,

> Several crew members said they'd never been on a happier location. Four of them ended up marrying local girls from San Antonio. . . . One was a waitress, another took reservations at the Holiday Inn.[41]

A scene from The Sugarland Express *starring Goldie Hawn as Lou Jean Poplin, the wife of an escaped convict.*

On the set of The Sugarland Express, *Steven Spielberg directs Goldie Hawn and William Atherton, who played Hawn's husband in the movie.*

Spielberg's confidence was also a factor in the film wrapping relatively quickly, only five days over schedule. It was edited during the summer, with postproduction finished by September. This ability to work efficiently was an important skill Spielberg had learned well. He remarks, "TV taught me to think on my feet."[42]

A Mixed Success

Sugarland was so innovative and exciting that Universal's executives were sure it would sweep the Oscars. It had daring camera angles and lighting techniques that are standard now but then seemed revolutionary for mainstream Hollywood. It was also the first Spielberg movie scored by John Williams, who has since contributed to many other Spielberg films.

The test audiences had a different reaction, however. They liked the first half, which was mostly comedy. But they were confused when the film took a serious turn in the second half. Spielberg recut the movie to eliminate some of the comedy and make the two halves fit together better.

When it opened in the spring of 1974, most critics loved it. Typical was the *New Yorker*'s Pauline Kael, who said that Spielberg "could be that rarity among directors, a born entertainer . . . this film is one of the most phenomenal debut films in the history of movies."[43]

Unfortunately, *Sugarland* was only a modest success at the box office and made only a modest profit. There is little agreement about the reasons. Some suggested that the title misdirected audiences into expecting a kid's movie. Others thought the oddball casting of Hawn, whom audiences wanted to see as a happy-go-lucky comedienne, was at fault. Spielberg himself blamed a confused promotional campaign, which left it unclear whether the film was a comedy or a drama.

By the time the movie was out, in any case, Spielberg was already well into a new project. He was on the Massachusetts island of Martha's Vineyard, preparing for another Zanuck/Brown picture. Its title was *Jaws*.

Chapter 4

The Blockbuster Years

I want the audience to go out of the theater screaming.
—Steven Spielberg on *Jaws*

IN THE OFFICES of Zanuck/Brown, Spielberg one day picked up a copy of Peter Benchley's novel *Jaws*, about a killer shark terrorizing a New England town. Spielberg was himself scared of water and sharks, and after reading the book he knew he could terrify audiences with a movie version. John Baxter writes, "He felt personally attacked by the shark, and wanted to strike back."[44]

Although *Jaws* was a smash hit that made Spielberg an international star, the production was a nightmare, running far over budget and behind schedule. While it was shooting, everyone connected with the film thought it was going to be a major failure.

Bruce

One of the major problems was the shark itself. After realizing the impossibility of effectively filming real sharks, Spielberg decided to create one.

Spielberg had three twenty-five-foot mechanical sharks built, each named Bruce in honor of Spielberg's lawyer. Each rode on an underwater crane, with thirteen technicians controlling it, and something in the complex systems always went wrong. One recurring glitch was that the sharks' eyes kept crossing.

Furthermore, the Bruces had never been tested in open water, and no one realized how badly their workings would corrode in salt water. Each night the machines had to be scrubbed, dried with hair dryers, and repaired. Michael Pye and Lynda

A photo taken during the making of Jaws *shows Spielberg reclining in the mouth of the mechanical shark named Bruce.*

Myles write, "Bruce alone put some $3.5 million onto the budget of *Jaws* by his awkward behavior; and he was only one of the technical troubles that the film faced."[45]

Other problems included the struggle to streamline the book's cluttered plot and the difficulty of filming on water. Spielberg could film only a few seconds on some days; on other days he got nothing.

As the schedule slipped and dozens of expensive workers waited, costs soared. The budget swelled from $4.5 million to $10 million, an enormous figure for the time. Rumors flew that Universal, the studio backing the project, was calling it quits. However, Sid Sheinberg, now the studio's head of production, loyally kept it going.

By the time shooting ended, morale was so low that Spielberg snuck off the island without saying goodbye to the crew. He later remarked that he had nightmares for three months afterward.

Despite this unpromising start, *Jaws'* unrelenting suspense made it an instant and massive success when it opened in June 1975. Within two months it set a new box-office record, passing *The Godfather* to become the most successful film in history.

Spigots

Jaws inspired a worldwide sharkmania, just as *Jurassic Park* would later inspire a global interest in dinosaurs. Bruce was on the cover of *Time. Jaws* discotheques opened. Ice cream parlors offered flavors like finilla. Stores sold strap-on styrofoam fins for swimmers. A more serious consequence was that the popularity of sportfishing expeditions for shark soared, which may have contributed to the endangerment of global shark populations.

The movie's success made international stars out of Spielberg and Richard Dreyfuss, the actor who played the marine-biologist hero. Though Spielberg's salary was relatively small, his percentage of the movie's profits made him a multimillionaire. Furthermore, he suddenly became a powerful figure in Hollywood, able to negotiate a huge budget for his next project. Producer Michael Phillips comments, "After *Jaws*, the money spigots opened."[46]

However, Spielberg felt that there had been little of himself in *Jaws*. He wanted his next project to be closer to his heart. Specifically, he wanted to do a big-budget remake of *Firelight*. Originally

Steven Spielberg takes a break with Jaws cast members, including (far right) Richard Dreyfuss. The incredible success of Jaws catapulted Spielberg into fame.

called *Watch the Skies,* this project was eventually retitled *Close Encounters of the Third Kind.*

The story involved a group of ordinary people who are mysteriously touched by UFO sightings, and a team of scientists who are tracking the extraterrestrials; its climax was a meeting between the humans and the aliens. Spielberg comments,

> I love juxtaposing . . . the cosmos with a real sort of suburban reality. . . . And it's essential for a film of this kind to base it here, on Earth. . . . You really have to believe in Earth before you can believe in flying saucers.[47]

Principal photography began late in 1975 in an abandoned military hangar in Alabama, one of the few buildings large enough to hold the massive soundstages Spielberg required. It was so immense that its air-conditioning units were sufficient to cool thirty large houses.

Richard Dreyfuss returned in the lead role, electrical lineman Roy Neary. Another important part, the childlike UFO investigator Lacombe, was played by a famous French director, François Truffaut.

The movie was made in deep secrecy. Spielberg didn't want his ideas stolen and made into a cheap, quick rip-off. Also, Spielberg

In a climactic scene from Close Encounters of the Third Kind, *people gather to witness the arrival of the alien ship.*

had had poor experiences with the press while making *Jaws;* reporters had been extremely intrusive on the supposedly closed set and had fueled a public battle between Spielberg and Benchley.

As a result, scripts for *Close Encounters* were numbered and given out daily in segments, so that only a few people knew the complete story. Spielberg himself was denied admission to the set one day because he forgot his ID badge.

Douglas Trumbull, who had worked on such classics as *2001: A Space Odyssey,* and cinematographer Vilmos Zsigmond were in charge of the film's elaborate special effects. Most of the effects had never been tried before, and the lengthy process of trial and error caused the film's budget to skyrocket. What began as a modest $4 million budget eventually ballooned to nearly $23 million.

Another Triumph

The entire crew, including Spielberg, became increasingly stressed by the rigors of production. Coproducer Julia Phillips, who took over sole production responsibilities when she broke up with husband, Michael Phillips, became so stressed that she turned to cocaine. Before the film was completed she became so erratic that she was relieved of her duties.

She was not the only nervous one. The accountants at Columbia, the studio behind the project, had calculated that *Close Encounters* would have to be one of the top eighteen moneymakers of all time just to break even. If it failed, the studio would be bankrupt. Writer-director John Milius, a friend and colleague of Spielberg's, commented, "It will either be the best Columbia film or it will be the last Columbia film."[48]

However, *Close Encounters* justified the worry and work. Enthusiastic audiences around the world made it into another massive hit. Spielberg received his first Oscar nomination for best director, one of eight nominations *Close Encounters* received. The movie was also praised by critics, who called it thought-provoking and deeply personal, even though it was mainstream entertainment. The *New Yorker's* Pauline Kael enthusiastically summed up the film's message as, "God is up there in a crystal-chandelier spaceship and He likes us."[49]

Spielberg refused to consider a sequel to *Close Encounters.* Instead, he edited the existing film and shot a few new scenes for a so-called special edition. This is the version generally available on video.

1941

For his next project, Spielberg chose a script by two young comedy writers, Robert Zemeckis and Bob Gale. *1941* was based on a true incident. Shortly after the attack on Pearl Harbor, a Japanese submarine fired on oil fields in California. The attack did little damage, but it scared many Americans into barely controlled panic. Spielberg and his colleagues turned this unlikely material into a free-for-all comedy about anti-Japanese hysteria.

Spielberg's previous two movies had been such hits that he was allowed a free hand with this production, and he demanded increasingly elaborate sets. No one was willing to tell the hotshot young director to restrain himself; Spielberg later ruefully called this his "Little General" period.

A full-size house was built so that it could fall off a cliff. Several vintage fighter planes were shot down at $1 million each.

Dan Akroyd and John Belushi star in 1941, *a comedy about a Japanese attack on California oil fields during World War II. The movie was criticized by reviewers and was a flop at the box office.*

The film's star, John Belushi, had an increasingly erratic work schedule that added to the expense and chaos. At a final cost of $31.5 million, $20 million over budget, *1941* became one of the most expensive Hollywood movies made up to that point.

When the movie opened late in 1979, the reviews were dev-astating; typical was the headline "Spielberg's Pearl Harbor." It was also a dismal box-office failure. Critics and audiences alike disliked the lumbering comedy about an essentially serious sub-ject. Spielberg himself had grown disenchanted with *1941* long before it was finished. When the film opened, he sadly told reporters, "I'll spend the rest of my life disowning this movie."[50]

Spielberg needed another hit fast if he wanted to bounce back from the embarrassment of *1941*. He found it in a project he'd been developing with his old friend George Lucas.

Back in the spring of 1977, Lucas had invited Spielberg to Hawaii as *Star Wars* opened. Both directors preferred staying away from Los Angeles to avoid the stress of a new opening.

One day, while the two were building a room-sized sand castle on a Hawaiian beach, Lucas talked about an idea he had for a new movie. It would combine the cliff-hanger adventure serials of his childhood with the dashing style of James Bond movies. The hero would lead a dual life: mild-mannered, acad-emic archaeologist and swashbuckling, slightly shady hero.

Spielberg loved it. Lucas was interested only in producing, so Spielberg offered to direct. He remarks:

> George Lucas is . . . a business genius, as well as a great conceptualizer, and I'm much more of a hard-working drone. I enjoy rolling up my sleeves and getting into it. I think George has fun thinking up ideas and then sitting back and saying, "OK, go off and make it. It's your movie now."[51]

Tight Budget

With screenwriter Lawrence Kasdan, the pair hammered out the details. They called their hero Indiana, after Lucas's wife's dog, and created a tale about the Ark of the Covenant, the holiest of Jewish relics. The story was called *Raiders of the Lost Ark*.

Michael Eisner, the head of Paramount, took on the project, but insisted on reasonable costs. Spielberg and Lucas faced stiff penalties if they went over the $20 million budget; if they stayed within it, they would receive large bonuses and a sizable percentage of the profits.

This deal was fine with Lucas, a conservative and disciplined producer. Spielberg was also eager to show he could make a high-quality movie within a tight budget. His last project, he said, had taught him that "creative compromise is more challenging than the blank cheque-book." [52]

Raiders was, in fact, the first Spielberg feature to come in under budget and on schedule. It was also an unqualified success. Its worldwide take, over $363 million, made it the highest-grossing picture in Paramount's history to date. Its financial and artistic success helped restore the director's reputation. Furthermore, the movie made a superstar out of Harrison Ford, who had been picked to play Indy only after Tom Selleck, the original choice, was unable to get away from his TV commitments.

The film was nominated for eight Oscars, including Spielberg's second for directing, and received five awards, all in technical categories. Typical of the critical reaction, meanwhile, was that of Vincent Canby of the *New York Times*, who called it "one of the most deliriously funny, ingenious and stylish American adventure movies ever made." [53]

Relationships

During the making of *Raiders*, two key people began working with Spielberg. Frank Marshall was the film's producer (Lucas was its executive producer) and Kathleen Kennedy was Spielberg's assistant. Marshall and Kennedy later married and became Spielberg's chief producers throughout the 1980s.

Spielberg had also formed another important new relationship. While working on *Close Encounters*, the director had one morning remarked, "I met a heartbreaker last night." [54]

She was Amy Irving, the actress daughter of a well-known theatrical director, Jules Irving. Irving quickly became Spielberg's first serious romance. Only a few months after director Brian de Palma introduced them, the couple moved in together,

Spielberg's success with Raiders of the Lost Ark *(top) was marred by his breakup with Amy Irving (bottom).*

buying a spacious home in Coldwater Canyon and bringing along a cook, Spielberg's cocker spaniel, and two parrots.

By the time Spielberg shot *Raiders*, however, the bond between the two was fraying. The main problem was that Irving felt stifled at being "Steven's girlfriend," rather than being considered on her own merits. She worried that her career was suffering because she was considered only an adjunct to a bigger celebrity.

When she moved out in 1980, the breakup devastated Spielberg. He dated a number of other women but could not form a lasting relationship. He told reporters he was going through a traumatic time of growing up that he'd missed because of his obsessive work habits. He remarked, "I'm experiencing delayed adolescence. I suffer like I'm sixteen. It's a miracle I haven't sprouted acne again."[55]

E.T.

Raiders had been fun to make, but once again it had not come from Spielberg's heart. He remarks, "I took the movie as seriously as I took a barrel of popcorn."[56]

While on location in Tunisia for *Raiders*, a more personal project took shape. The director, far from close friends, soothed his loneliness, as he had done as a boy, by inventing an imaginary friend. In this case it was a tender-hearted alien who treasured the relationship as much as Spielberg did.

Spielberg and screenwriter Melissa Mathison, visiting her future husband Harrison Ford on the *Raiders* set, began elaborating this idea. The alien evolved into a botanist accidentally stranded while collecting plants on Earth; the boy became Elliott, the child of a broken marriage. Their relationship formed the backbone of *E.T.: The Extraterrestrial.* Spielberg says, "*E.T.* was conceived by me as a love story, the love between a ten-year-old boy and a nine-hundred-year-old alien."[57]

Back in the States, Spielberg shot the story on a relatively small budget of $10 million. *E.T.* used only minor special effects; the humans were as important as the memorable alien created by creature maker Carlo Rambaldi. With this film, Spielberg demonstrated a knack for working with child actors, bringing out their strengths by treating them as equals. Henry Thomas as Elliott and Drew Barrymore as Gertie gave particularly powerful performances.

Champ

When the film was released in June 1982, not everyone liked its message, a bittersweet mixture of love, hope, longing, and sadness. British critic Kenneth Taylor thought the movie was "nauseating, sentimental rubbish."[58]

Most critics, though, responded ecstatically. Roger Ebert wrote, "It is one of the rare movies that brush away our cautions and win our hearts." Michael Sragow agreed: "[Y]ou feel that Spielberg has, for the first time, put his breathtaking technical skills at the service of his deepest feelings."[59]

Audiences agreed. At the box office, *E.T.* sailed beyond the record-holder, *Star Wars*, and earned an astonishing $399 million

Steven Spielberg and Drew Barrymore on the set of E.T. Spielberg is known for his aptitude for working with child actors.

just in the United States. This was the biggest domestic box-office take in history, and E.T. became a worldwide hero.

Neil Diamond wrote a song inspired by E.T.'s glowing heart-light, Michael Jackson narrated an album about him, and there were dozens of authorized E.T. products. Spielberg helped plan Universal Studios's E.T. ride. The director was invited to screen the film for a number of dignitaries at special functions, including the president, the queen of England, and officials at the United Nations, who gave Spielberg a special peace medal. E.T. even made the cover of *Rolling Stone.*

The film's overwhelming popularity reflected the simplicity of its message, which anyone could understand. Writer Martin Amis describes his first viewing:

Towards the end of *E.T.*, barely able to support my own grief and bewilderment, I turned and looked down the aisle at my fellow sufferers: executive, black dude, Japanese businessman, punk, hippie, mother, teenager, child. Each face was a mask of tears.[60]

Other Productions

Overlapping *E.T.* was another Spielberg project, *Poltergeist*. This grim horror movie, about ghosts invading a suburban home, represented the flip side of E.T.'s sweetness.

Officially *Poltergeist* was produced and written by Spielberg and directed by Tobe Hooper. According to many sources, however, Spielberg was in effect the director. He was on the set almost every day and made most of the important decisions. According to the film's music composer, Jerry Goldsmith, "Hooper said 'Action' and that's the last thing he did."[61]

Another project from this period was tinged with tragedy. Co-produced by Spielberg and director John Landis, *Twilight Zone— The Movie* had four segments, including ones directed by Spielberg and Landis. During the shooting of Landis's segment, a damaged helicopter fell and killed actor Vic Morrow and two child actors.

Charges of involuntary manslaughter were brought against Landis and four others. The defendants were acquitted, but the trial revealed that the children had been illegally hired and Landis had violated safety laws.

In addition to its tragic deaths, the incident was terrible publicity for Spielberg. He was never directly involved, and authorities concluded that he was not linked to the accident or the illegal practices. Nonetheless, because Spielberg was a big name, he was hounded by reporters for months.

Spielberg tried to distance himself. At one point he tried to remove his name from the project, but his lawyers felt that doing so would be an admission of guilt. Spielberg has since maintained almost complete silence about the affair; in a rare public comment he said in 1983,

> A movie is a fantasy. No movie is worth dying for. I think people are standing up much more now than ever before to producers and directors who ask too much. If something isn't safe, it's the right and responsibility of every actor or crew member to yell, "Cut!"[62]

Temple of Doom

When Spielberg and Lucas made *Raiders*, they had a "gentleman's agreement" that if it was successful they would make two more. *Indiana Jones and the Temple of Doom*, the second install-ment, was shot in the spring and summer of 1983.

The filmmakers did not want to repeat themselves, and the new movie was much darker than the lighthearted *Raiders*. The story, about a village of enslaved children in India, included scenes of people being burned alive and a man's beating heart being ripped out. Spielberg comments, "You could say that the villains in the last film were evil, but they dealt in simple force. In this movie, our villains deal in black magic, torture and slav-ery. So they're *real* bad."[63]

Winning and Losing

In their book *Steven Spielberg*, Donald R. Mott and Cheryl McAllister Saunders reprint this excerpt from an interview at the time *Temple of Doom* was released, in which Spielberg talks about the problems of sequels.

[T]he danger in making a sequel is that you can never satisfy everyone. If you give people the same movie with different scenes, they say, "Why weren't you more original?" But if you give them the same character in another fantastic adventure, but with a different tone, you risk disappointing the other half of the audience, who just wanted a carbon copy of the first film with a different girl and a different bad guy. So you win and you lose both ways.

Actors Ke Huy Quan, Kate Capshaw, and Harrison Ford in Indiana Jones and the Temple of Doom.

Many parents and critics hated the violence. One reviewer said that taking a kid to *Temple of Doom* was "a cinematic form of child abuse." Spielberg's supporters responded by saying that the director had often been accused of going too far in the opposite direction, of being artificially sweet and gentle. Where, they wondered, was a happy medium?

The violence in *Temple of Doom* and *Poltergeist* was largely responsible for the creation of a new rating by the Motion Picture Association of America. Previously, movie ratings had gone from G to PG to R, but now a new rating was added: PG-13, meaning no one under thirteen could see the film without a parent or guardian.

Ecstasy and Grief

For Spielberg, the early 1980s had been a period of great ups and downs. In the spring of 1983 he commented, "This has been the most interesting year of my film career. It has mixed the best, the success of *E.T.*, with the worst, the *Twilight Zone* tragedy. A mixture of ecstasy and grief."[64]

More broadly, movies with Spielberg's name on them had a part in changing the course of Hollywood, by helping to usher in the age of the blockbuster. As this age moved in, the fortunes of an entire studio could rise or fall on a single big film. Steven Farber and Marc Green note, "[T]he blockbuster movie was . . . born in the 1970s. Suddenly one hit picture could gross more than the entire body of work turned out by [earlier directors such as] John Ford or Frank Capra."[65]

Many observers of the movie industry were dismayed by this turn of events. They felt that smaller, more original films suffered when so much money rode on a few epics, because the riskier projects were dropped in favor of bland but surefire hits.

Spielberg himself seemed to agree. The next period in his career marked a move away from crowd-pleasing "popcorn movies" and toward more thoughtful, issue-oriented projects.

Chapter 5

New Directions, New Family

The next UFO I want to see is the one that sits down in my backyard and takes me on an all-expense-paid trip to the Virgin Islands.
— Steven Spielberg, after supervising one too many special effects

Before I had Max, I made films about kids; now that I have one, I'll probably start making films about adults.
— Steven Spielberg, after the birth of his first child

SPIELBERG WAS OFFERED several executive positions, including head of the Disney studios, following the overwhelming success of *E.T.* He declined them all, and instead formed his own production company in 1983. Spielberg used it to expand his artistic and business horizons, developing and producing movies that he did not have time to direct himself.

In a nod to his early breakthrough film, Spielberg called the new company Amblin' Entertainment. (The apostrophe was later dropped.) Martin Amis visited the company's offices on the Paramount lot and wryly noted Spielberg's phenomenal productivity: "His office now bears the nostalgic logo, Amblin' Productions— though these days Sprintin' would be nearer the mark."[66]

Amblin's first official project was a movie called *Wargames*, and although Amblin eventually decided not to make the film, the occasion was fruitful for Spielberg. He formed a friendship with the movie's co-writer, Walter Parkes, who later became a close collaborator.

Amblin's structure also protected and supported the director, insulating him from day-to-day dealings and putting restraints on his most unrealistic daydreams. *Time* magazine's Richard Corliss noted at the time that most of this protection came from Kathleen Kennedy and Frank Marshall:

> They share executive producer credits on the films [Spielberg] presents; they keep four sharp eyes on a dozen or so film projects; they grease the tracks that connect Steven with the studios and the press; they act as a DEW [distant early warning] line to monitor the unguided missiles of his imagination.[67]

The Color Purple

Spielberg's reputation had been built as a maker of big, spectacular movies that often appealed more to kids than adults. In that light, the movie that Spielberg chose as his next directing project was unusual: a film version of Alice Walker's Pulitzer Prize–winning novel, *The Color Purple*.

The Color Purple is a small, serious story. The main character is Celie, a poor black woman in rural Georgia earlier in this century who suffers terribly at the hands of her violent, cruel father and her husband. In telling Celie's story, the book vividly depicts such intense, controversial topics as incest, lesbianism, and physical and mental abuse.

Purple's underlying themes include strong statements of black identity, oppression, and feminist principles. Many observers wondered: could a white, male director of effects-heavy films do the job? *Newsweek*'s David Ansen commented that the idea of Spielberg tackling *The Color Purple* was "as improbable as, say, [Italian art-movie director Michelangelo] Antonioni directing a James Bond movie."[68]

Not from Mars

Spielberg related to the book's themes of oppression and alienation because of his Jewishness, a topic he had not often talked about or illustrated. Few people outside his close circle, therefore, could have guessed how powerfully he might respond to *The Color Purple*.

Kathleen Kennedy introduced Spielberg to the book. He recalls:

She [said], "You know it's a black story. But that shouldn't bother you, because you're Jewish and essentially you share similarities in your upbringing and your heritage." I had some anti-Semitic experiences when I was growing up that Kathleen knew about.[69]

To reporters, Spielberg said that he wanted to challenge himself with something new, to flex a different set of movie-making muscles. He added that there was no reason why a white director shouldn't be interested in the material.

Privately, however, Spielberg did at first express some doubt that he was the right person for the job. He asked music producer Quincy Jones, who was also one of the executive producers of *Purple*, whether a black man or woman wouldn't be more suitable. Jones reassured him by saying, "You didn't have to come from Mars to do *E.T.*, did you?"[70]

"Wake Up, Stupid"

Spielberg shot *Purple* without storyboards, something he had done before only with *E.T.* He felt that elaborately preplanning every shot hindered the telling of *Purple*'s emotional, personal, character-driven story. The spontaneity of shooting with some improvisation, he believed, brought out the best in himself and his actors.

Largely because of this, the acting in *Purple* is some of the strongest in any Spielberg movie. Veteran actors like Danny Glover and Margaret Avery gave memorable performances; Oprah Winfrey, then a local talk-show host in Chicago, also turned in a solid film debut.

But the film's highlight was a radiant performance by Whoopi Goldberg, a then-unknown standup comic making her first appearance in film. Many observers feel that Goldberg's portrayal of Celie's development—from a timid, abused, and repressed farm girl into a strong, self-reliant woman—was one of the most auspicious debuts in recent film history.

The actress was brought to Spielberg's attention by author Walker, who was familiar with Goldberg's one-woman, multi-character show. When Spielberg offered her the role of Celie,

Goldberg resisted; she was more interested in Sofia, the part taken by Winfrey. She recalls: "And then I realized that Steven Spielberg's sitting there trying to convince me to be in his movie. And it was like, "Wake up, stupid. Say *yes*."[71]

Good and Bad Reactions

The Color Purple opened on Spielberg's birthday, December 18, 1985. Most of the reviews were positive, and thirty-three critics put it in their top ten lists for the year. The film also did surprisingly well at the box office, considering it was a "small" and serious movie rather than a blockbuster. It took in $142.7 million worldwide, far more than its $15 million budget.

Some reviewers and members of the public were not impressed, however. Many saw the switch in styles as a cynical move by Spielberg to snag a Best-Director Oscar.

Another criticism was that Spielberg had made *Purple* artificially glossy and upbeat. The *Washington Post*'s Rita Kempley, for instance, wrote that he turned its setting, rural Georgia, into "a pastoral paradise that makes Dorothy Gale's Kansas farm look like a slum."[72] Spielberg replied by pointing out that the movie's look had been based on photos of the home of Alice Walker's well-off, landowning grandparents.

Some members of the African American community also objected to the film's harsh representation of black men. Finally, critics again brought up the question of Spielberg's credentials. *L.A. Weekly* reviewer John Powers complained that Spielberg "finds it harder to imagine black people than spacemen."[73] Spielberg reacted to such criticism by saying, "This is a human story, and the film is about human beings. . . .

Whoopi Goldberg made an exemplary film debut performance as Celie in The Color Purple.

Spielberg directs Whoopi Goldberg in The Color Purple, *which received mixed reviews and did not win any Oscars, though it was nominated for eleven.*

This is a movie about the triumph of the spirit—and spirit and soul never had any racial boundaries."[74]

Criticism was also dealt out at the Oscars. Although nominated for eleven awards, including Best Picture, Best Actress, and two for Best Supporting Actress, *Purple* did not receive a single one.

Although he was hurt and angered, Spielberg was unruffled in public, telling reporters he was "a moviemaker, not a belly-acher." Many felt that Spielberg was being punished simply because of his success. Director Richard Brooks, a friend of Spielberg's, comments, "He's the most successful director in the world. I guess when you get up that high, you're bound to find people who will throw stones at you."[75]

Personal Changes

Along with the professional change of pace marked by his direction of *The Color Purple*, Spielberg's private life underwent major changes during this period.

During the 1980s he began to enjoy a more lavish lifestyle. This was largely due to the influence of a new mentor and father figure: Steve Ross, the stylish and charismatic chairman of Time Warner, the parent company of Warner Studios.

Ross convinced Spielberg to buy expensive real estate, including an apartment in Manhattan and an estate in East Hampton, New York. He also encouraged the director to collect art and other items of significance. These purchases included $60,500 for one of the snow sleds from *Citizen Kane*, the masterpiece by another Hollywood wonder boy, Orson Welles.

Spielberg's romantic life also changed during this time. Since their breakup, Amy Irving had been active on Broadway and in movies, including an Oscar-nominated role in Barbra Streisand's *Yentl*. She had lost her frustration over being simply "Steven's girlfriend" and was interested in rekindling their romance.

So was Spielberg. The relationship blossomed again, and together the couple bought a large hilltop estate in Pacific Palisades, one of Los Angeles's most exclusive neighborhoods.

When Irving became pregnant in the fall of 1984, she and Spielberg were delighted. Max Samuel Spielberg, whom his father called "my best production yet," was born in the summer of 1985. By a strange coincidence, Irving went into labor as Spielberg was shooting the childbirth scene in *The Color Purple*. Informed that Spielberg was on the set, Irving said, "Okay, tell him to come home and deliver *my* baby now."[76]

Hardworking Father

That November, Spielberg and Irving were married in a civil ceremony in Santa Fe, with her sister and their attorney as the only witnesses.

After a three-month honeymoon in Europe, Spielberg settled in as a husband and father. He promised to cut down on his hectic work schedule to spend more time with his family. But he nonetheless kept busy throughout the 1980s, and in addition to his own movies, he produced dozens of films and television shows.

Some of these were successful artistically and commercially. The best, such as the animated TV series *Animaniacs* and the films *Back to the Future* and *Who Framed Roger Rabbit*, were commercial hits that were also intelligent productions appealing to both kids and adults. Not everything Amblin produced was as successful, however. Among its lesser productions were the television shows *seaQuest DSV* and *Amazing Stories* and the films *Continental Divide* and *I Wanna Hold Your Hand.*

Some of Amblin's projects were developed from ideas generated by outside writers and producers, but many came directly from Spielberg's fertile imagination. He was famous for enthusiastically shooting off ideas at random, and it was often up to his associates to decide which were worth pursuing. Frank Marshall remarked during this period, "He has an idea every thirteen seconds. I have to figure out how serious they are. If he wants to do something, I have to figure out how to make it possible financially." [77]

Empire of the Sun

In the mid-1980s, one of Spielberg's idols, director David Lean, was considering a film of J. G. Ballard's semiautobiographical book *Empire of the Sun.*

Spielberg's movie Empire of the Sun *was based on a book by the same name. Here, Spielberg chats with the film's stars, Christian Bale (left) and John Malkovitch.*

This novel is about the experiences of a boy during Japan's occupation of China in World War II. Jim Graham, obsessed with flying and airplanes, lives with his well-off English family in Shanghai, China. When the Japanese invade, Jim is separated from his parents and sent to a prison camp, where he learns to survive under brutal conditions.

Spielberg was initially set to produce the picture, but Lean dropped the project in favor of another. Spielberg then decided to do it himself and commissioned a screenplay from the distinguished Czech-British playwright Tom Stoppard.

Spielberg hoped to combine Lean's epic style of storytelling with his own interpretation of the book's themes of survival, loss, separation, and the pain of growing up. The setting of Shanghai was also significant for Spielberg because some of his father's relatives had fled there from Russia. The director recalls,

> From the moment I read the novel, I secretly wanted to do it myself. [In it, a] child saw things through a man's eyes as opposed to a man discovering things through the child in him. It was just the reverse of what I felt was [in previous pictures] my credo.[78]

Shooting in Shanghai

Filming took place in Spain, where a replica of a Japanese prison camp was built, and on location in Shanghai. The Chinese shoot was the first Hollywood movie to be filmed extensively in China, following a year of negotiations between Chinese officials and Kennedy and Marshall.

When it opened in December 1987, *Empire* received mixed reviews from the critics, who mostly seemed perplexed. They agreed that the film was magnificently filmed and well-acted, singling out a powerful performance by John Malkovitch as a shady American named Basie. But they were baffled that Spielberg, who had always sentimentalized childhood, would make a film in which a boy survives by becoming a con man and black marketeer.

Some were also dismayed by the movie's somber tone. They felt that Spielberg should stick with effects-heavy extravaganzas, and they ridiculed his efforts to make serious movies. A critic

Whatever Works

This anecdote, told by assistant director David Tomblin about the first day's shooting for *Empire of the Sun,* in Joseph McBride's *Steven Spielberg: A Biography,* illustrates Spielberg's increasing willingness to improvise on the spot and to be satisfied with what's available.

> [I] plotted out all the crowd movement and everything, and I planned to keep the road clear so there could be traffic movement. I drew it all out and told everyone what to do. Then five thousand people suddenly flooded the road. I went crazy. I said to Steven, "Oh, Jesus, it's all gone wrong!" He said, "Looks great." So I said, "Roll the cameras. Action!" He was happy with how it looked, and I wasn't going to argue with five thousand people. He's very good like that. He's not pedantic. Whatever is there, he makes it work.

for the Los Angeles *Herald-Examiner* wrote sarcastically, "I hope Steven Spielberg's *Empire of the Sun* wins him that damn Oscar so he goes back to making movies that give real and lasting pleasure to people." [79]

Empire was a commercial disappointment as well. It made only $66.7 million worldwide, less even than *1941.* This was still a small profit, however, since the movie had cost about $30 million and advertising costs were not enormous. As for the Oscars, *Empire* was nominated for six, all in craft categories, and did not win any.

Last Crusade

Spielberg's next film fulfilled his "gentleman's agreement" with George Lucas to complete the Indy Jones trilogy.

For Spielberg, shooting *Indiana Jones and the Last Crusade* meant dropping *Rain Man,* a project he had been developing for years with actors Dustin Hoffman and Tom Cruise. (With another director, *Rain Man* became a major hit and a multiple Oscar winner.) Spielberg remarks that his promise to Lucas took precedence: "[W]ith great regret, because I really wanted to work with Dustin and Tom, I stepped down from that movie." [80]

Having used Jewish and Hindu treasures in the first two Indy movies, Spielberg, Lucas, and screenwriter Jeffrey Boam created a tale involving the most sacred Christian relic: the Holy Grail, the cup that Jesus is said to have used at the Last Supper. The story also involved Indy's quest for reconciliation with his estranged father. Spielberg recalls, "I wanted to do Indy in pursuit of his father, sharing his father's dream, and in the course of searching for their dreams, they rediscover each other."[81]

Spielberg suggested for the father the ruggedly suave Scottish actor Sean Connery, best known as the original James Bond. This was a sly touch, since the Indy Jones series had been created to both honor and outdo Bond. Indeed, there was much the same about the two heroes, as Connery wryly notes: "Aside from the fact that Indiana Jones is not as well-dressed as James Bond, the main difference between them is [that] Indiana deals with women shyly."[82]

Critics generally felt that *Last Crusade* was rousing entertainment, like the first Indy movie, that avoided the racist overtones and violence of the second installment. Audiences agreed: after it opened in May 1989, *Last Crusade* collected $494.7 million worldwide—Spielberg's biggest hit since *E.T.* Perhaps just as importantly, it had been fun to make—a welcome change emotionally from the two exhausting films Spielberg had done before.

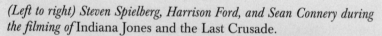

(Left to right) Steven Spielberg, Harrison Ford, and Sean Connery during the filming of Indiana Jones and the Last Crusade.

Always

A desire to return to more personal filmmaking, and to make a nostalgic journey to a beloved story, inspired Spielberg's next project.

Always was a remake of *A Guy Named Joe*, a 1943 film starring Spencer Tracy. Spielberg had watched it often on television as a child and young adult, and it remained one of his favorites. He has often remarked that it was the second film, after *Bambi*, that made him cry.

The story concerned a fighter pilot who loses his life, then returns to earth as an angel to help his true love work through her grief. Realizing that he has to let her continue living, he helps her find happiness with another man.

Spielberg brought the story to the present time and set it among aerial forest firefighters. As usual, the movie was visually spectacular and well-cast. Richard Dreyfuss, returning as Spielberg's on-screen persona, played the pilot with a mixture of gusto and bittersweet sorrow. Holly Hunter portrayed his tough, brave girlfriend. John Goodman was the pilot's loyal friend, and Brad Johnson was the handsome but dull pilot Hunter falls for.

Unfortunately, *Always* was not overly popular, critically or at the box office. Some observers speculate that its disappointing performance hinged on its sentimental themes of love, loss, and sacrifice. These appealed to families coming to terms with their own sacrifices during the war years but not with audiences and critics of the late 1980s. Although some critics considered *Always* an unjustly neglected gem, Vincent Canby of the *New York Times* spoke for the majority when he wrote,

> Though the story calls out for simplicity, it unfolds in an atmosphere of forced laughter and forced tears. Gentle and moving as it means to be, there is barely a scene that wouldn't have worked better with less fanfare.[83]

Troubled Marriage

Spielberg had tried hard to concentrate on family after his son's birth, but his compulsion toward nonstop work had always been great. Despite an intense desire for a stable family after his parents'

A still from Always *shows Richard Dreyfuss as an angel observing the woman he loves (Holly Hunter) with her new love (Brad Johnson).*

traumatic breakup, Spielberg apparently could not do what was needed to sustain his own.

For her part, Amy Irving still felt frustration at being considered only a wife. When starting her career, she had been known as the daughter of a famous stage director, Jules Irving. She told friends that she didn't want to end her career known as the wife of another famous director.

Irving felt constrained in other ways as well. She was uncomfortable caring for residences in Malibu, Pacific Palisades, East Hampton, and Manhattan. The constant presence of egotistical movie stars at parties was also not her style: "I felt like a politician's wife. There were certain things 'expected of' me that definitely weren't me." Furthermore, she had to turn down choice roles, such as Mozart's wife in the film *Amadeus,* because of the demands of motherhood. "I had a baby," she says, "and lost my place in line."[84]

Spielberg and Irving had tried to alternate projects so the family could be together. This proved difficult to maintain, however.

When Spielberg was obligated to shoot *The Last Crusade* in Europe, for instance, Irving was offered a prestigious role on Broadway. For a time, they flew back and forth across the ocean to visit, but that schedule proved impossible and the relationship grew increasingly strained.

Hook

After wrapping *Always*, Spielberg returned to a beloved childhood story but used a more lavish style of storytelling than he had used for *Always*.

He had always loved J. M. Barrie's play about Peter Pan, the little boy who refused to grow up. Many of his friends and colleagues, in fact, insisted that the director himself had never really grown up. The movie *Big*, about a high-spirited boy trapped in a man's body, was co-written by Spielberg's sister Anne, and some observers speculate that it was affectionately based on Steven.

For years, Spielberg had considered a live-action version of *Peter Pan*, starring Michael Jackson as Peter and Dustin Hoffman as Captain Hook. This project never reached fruition; by the time Jackson and Hoffman became available, Spielberg was a father and had cut back on his schedule. Referring to the technique used to film human actors before special visual effects are added, he remarks, "I didn't want to . . . have seven kids on wires in front of blue screens swinging around. I wanted to be home as a dad, not a surrogate dad." [85]

When Spielberg did decide to make a film about Peter Pan, he picked a script that took a new look at the story. Jim V. Hart's screenplay concerned a workaholic yuppie who ignores his own children—and has forgotten that he once was the real Peter Pan. When his children are kidnapped by Captain Hook, he must become Peter again to rescue them.

Once again, Spielberg had found a story that focused on many of his own concerns: a troubled relationship between father and son, the loss and rediscovery of innocence, and the problems of a workaholic who ignores the life around him. Bob Hoskins, the British actor who played Smee, remarks, "*Peter Pan* is about lost childhood. *Hook* is about lost fatherhood." [86]

Not Laguna Beach

Hook was funded by the Japanese electronics firm Sony, which had just bought the Columbia-Tristar studio and was happy to underwrite a lavish production. Originally budgeted at $48 million, the film's final cost has been estimated at closer to $80 million. Spielberg defended the cost by saying,

> We all have expectations for Neverland, so we needed to put our heads together to create a Neverland that you could believe in, that would look like Neverland and not just Laguna Beach." [87]

Despite its eye-popping sets and all-star cast including Dustin Hoffman, Robin Williams, and Julia Roberts, however, the critics pounded *Hook* when it opened in December 1991. They thought it worked too hard to be whimsical, and they ironically pointed out that it was the most expensive movie ever made about simple values. The *New Yorker* noted, "Its tricks feel

Steven Spielberg on the set of Hook *with Julia Roberts and Robin Williams. Though the movie received negative reviews, it brought in a sizeable income.*

strained; we're constantly aware of the backbreaking effort it is taking to produce them, and that's no kind of magic at all."[88]

The Academy again ignored Spielberg, nominating *Hook* for five Oscars in technical categories but giving it none, and turnout at the box office in the United States was unimpressive. However, the film did well overseas, bringing in a worldwide income of $288 million.

New Directions

The period of Spielberg's life spanning *The Color Purple* to *Hook* was an important transitional one, both personally and professionally.

Some critics and members of the public objected to his more serious movies; they wanted him to keep making pure escapism. Perhaps one part of Spielberg did want to continue doing that. However, he matured as a person and was also stretching his artistic boundaries.

He took on the responsibilities of marriage and fatherhood, although they proved difficult to sustain. At the same time, Spielberg also tried many different cinematic styles, from serious dramas to pulp adventures and spiritual love stories. In this way he blended an increasingly personal creative style with his already established gift for entertainment. He remarked at the release of *Empire,*

> I've had ten years, and a lot of success, in a certain genre of movie. Now I have to explore other forms, to shake myself out of what every artist fears, which is lethargy and apathy. I'm looking forward to a new and unusual ten years.[89]

Spielberg was, in short, experimenting with the methods and ideas that would lead him to *Schindler's List,* the movie that many consider his masterpiece. He was also moving into a period that would provide him with a stable home life and a renewed sense of family and religion.

Chapter 6

Maturity at Home and on the Screen

Part of me is afraid I will be remembered for the money my films have made, rather than the films themselves. Do people remember the gold medal, or do they remember what the gold medal was won for?

—Steven Spielberg

In APRIL 1989, after three and a half years of marriage and months of speculation in the Hollywood rumor mill, Steven Spielberg and Amy Irving publicly announced their divorce. They agreed to share custody of young Max. Irving also received a large monetary settlement. This amount has never been made public, but it was probably about $100 million, roughly half of Spielberg's net worth at the time.

Both parties have generally maintained a public silence about the painful breakup. On occasion, though, Spielberg has remarked that the two most difficult times in his life were during his parents' divorce and his own.

Enter Kate Capshaw

In the months preceding the official divorce announcement, the Hollywood gossip grapevine had linked both Spielberg and Irving romantically with several others. In the case of Spielberg, it was most often with actress Kate Capshaw.

They met when Capshaw had played Willie, the dizzy blonde in *Temple of Doom*. The actress had hated her whiny, screaming role, but she had immediately been attracted to the director.

Apparently the feeling was mutual. Spielberg was involved with Irving, however, so the flirtation did not become serious. Later, as Spielberg's marriage was breaking up, he and Capshaw renewed their romance and she moved into his Malibu house.

The relationship was not without problems. As the prospect of marriage grew closer, Spielberg suggested a prenuptial agreement (a legal plan clarifying the division of property in case of a divorce). Irving had received so much of his money that the director wanted to limit his losses in case his second marriage also failed.

The details of this agreement have remained private. Reportedly, Spielberg offered to pay Capshaw $2 million. She countered with $2 million for each year the marriage lasted, up to five years. The need to create such cold arrangements was extremely stressful, and for a time Capshaw moved out. By early 1990, however, the two had come to an agreement.

Plenty of Kids

Capshaw already had a daughter, Jessica, from a previous marriage. During her time apart from Spielberg, Capshaw adopted

Kate Capshaw and Steven Spielberg (pictured here with Capshaw's daughter, Jessica) were married in 1991.

another child, an infant named Theo. Their first child together, a daughter named Sasha, was born in May 1990. Three more have since joined the couple's extended family: Sawyer, Destry, and another adopted child, Mikaela. This brings the total, including Max, to seven.

Once they were firmly due to be married, Capshaw began studies to convert to Judaism from Methodism, the religion in which she had been raised. Capshaw says she was attracted to Judaism by its strong commitment to the family. She remarks, "It was very important to me that our home be a Jewish home, that our children were raised Jewish." [90]

Spielberg and Capshaw were married in October 1991 in a Jewish ceremony at their East Hampton home. Among the celebrants were many of their friends and associates, including Steve Ross, Barbra Streisand, Richard Dreyfuss, Harrison Ford, Dustin Hoffman, and Robin Williams.

The marriage has been, by all accounts, happy and stable. Spielberg's friends and associates feel that the relationship has given him a new sense of security, calmness, and balance. His longtime associate Kathleen Kennedy says, "He has a personal confidence now and isn't trying to prove anything to himself anymore." [91]

Jurassic Park

One day in 1989, Spielberg met with Michael Crichton, the writer and director whom he had first met during his apprentice days on the Universal lot. They were discussing plans for a jointly produced television series, *E.R.*

Spielberg casually asked Crichton what else he was working on, and the writer told him about a novel-in-progress called *Jurassic Park*. Borrowing from an earlier film Crichton wrote and directed, *Westworld,* and from Sir Arthur Conan Doyle's 1912 novel *The Lost World* (a title Crichton would also borrow later), Crichton's book posed provocative questions: What if scientists could create living dinosaurs with DNA technology? And what if the creatures were put in a commercial wildlife park?

Spielberg fell in love with the idea. He sought the movie rights when the book came out in 1990, but competition from other directors prompted a bidding war. Spielberg won by agreeing to

pay Crichton $1.5 million, plus
another half-million for a screenplay version and a large percentage of the movie's profits.

Making the Dinosaurs

Preproduction began in June
1990, but the complexities of
turning *Jurassic* into a believ-
able film required a longer
time frame than usual. Principal photography in Hawaii did
not start until August 1992. It
wrapped twelve days ahead of
schedule, despite an interrup-
tion from Hurricane Iniki. The
crew and cast rode the storm

*Spielberg used computer graphics
to create the ferocious tyrannosaur
in* Jurassic Park.

out in the ballroom of the Westin Kauai Hotel as Spielberg kept
them entertained with ghost stories.

The film's final costs were high, and a reliable figure is difficult
to determine. Estimates vary as high as $95 million, though $60 million may be closer to the actual figure. The main reason for the
unusually high costs involved the complex computer graphic imag-
ing (CGI) required for creating realistic dinosaurs.

Spielberg had first experimented with mechanical models
and had ordered full-sized ambulatory robots. He also tried animatronic models, like the shark in *Jaws*, and tested a process of
filming miniatures called go-motion. All of these, however, were
limited and unrealistic.

The director had not at first seriously considered computer
graphics, since what he had seen of the process was too crude.
But as other techniques proved unsatisfactory, the film's effects
supervisor, Dennis Muren, proposed giving CGI another try.

The results were far more striking than anyone had expected.
When a miniature maker, Phil Tippett, first saw Muren's CGI
tests, he reportedly looked at Spielberg and said, "I think I'm
extinct." Spielberg apparently incorporated this wisecrack into the
movie, giving the line to chaos theoretician Ian Malcolm.

In the end, Spielberg used a combination of animatronic and CGI images to get the effects he wanted. Although the fifty-four CGI sequences used in the final version of the movie account for a total of only six and a half minutes of screen time, they became *Jurassic*'s most famous and talked-about moments.

Another Smash

Besides being the sort of fast-moving and exciting story Spielberg loved, *Jurassic Park* explored some of his favorite issues: father figures, children in danger, and technology's dual promise of wonder and terror.

Jurassic also explored another theme important to Spielberg's later movies: the frustrations and rewards of parenting. Film critic Douglas Brode explains,

> If the young Spielberg made movies that glorified the joys of childhood [and] an adult's uneasiness about leaving such pleasures behind, the mature Spielberg makes movies about . . . reclaiming that wonderful child-like way of perceiving the world by sharing it with one's own child.[92]

Such themes clearly rang true with audiences as well. *Jurassic* was an instant hit when it opened in June 1993. In less than four months it surpassed the previous box-office record set by Spielberg's own *E.T.* and finished with a record worldwide gross of $913 million.

Jurassic's popularity sparked a global interest in dinosaurs comparable to the sharkmania once created by *Jaws*. Writer Jody Duncan notes, "*Jurassic Park* single-handedly incited a world-wide dinosaur craze."[93]

In the wake of such popularity, critical reaction seemed almost beside the point. Nonetheless, some reviewers criticized the movie's emphasis on special effects over human characters and deplored its commercialism. Critic David Thomson called it "comically bereft of any character or purpose except that of making marvels and money."[94]

As if in answer to such criticism, however, Spielberg was already preparing a very different sort of movie—one that was powerfully, shatteringly human.

Schindler

In 1982, Sid Sheinberg had bought the movie rights to a novel, *Schindler's Ark*, by an Australian writer, Thomas Keneally. The novel, renamed *Schindler's List* for its American publication, had won the Booker Prize, the most prestigious literary prize in the British Commonwealth.

Schindler's List was a fictionalized version of a true story dating from the Holocaust, when six million European Jews were killed as part of the Nazi plan to exterminate those who did not meet their standards of race or religion. Its pivotal character was Oskar Schindler, a Czech-born manufacturer.

Schindler began the war as a member of the Nazi Party and a shrewd profiteer who benefited from the virtual slave labor of Jews imprisoned in Nazi "forced labor" camps. However, as he

A scene from Spielberg's movie Schindler's List *shows Oskar Schindler (played by Liam Neeson) and Itzhak Stern (actor Ben Kingsley) compiling a list of Jewish workers to be placed under Schindler's protection.*

observed the increasingly brutal treatment of Jews by the Nazis, Schindler experienced a wrenching change of heart.

As the war raged, Schindler secretly saved eleven hundred Jews from almost certain death in the concentration camps. He did this by "buying" the workers with his personal fortune, insisting that they were skilled and indispensable laborers. He set them up in a phony munitions factory in Poland and managed to maintain the illusion until the end of the war.

A Change of Heart

Sheinberg had bought the rights to this story with Spielberg in mind, but Spielberg kept postponing his involvement. He later said that he did not feel ready to deal effectively with a subject so close to his own background; his family members' memories of the Holocaust were still vivid.

As a result, the project was considered by various other directors, including Martin Scorsese and Sydney Pollack. Hollywood legend Billy Wilder, who had fled Austria when Hitler came to power and had lost most of his family in the concentration camps, was approached. So was Roman Polanski, who had partly grown up in the Jewish ghetto of Krakow and who had lost his mother at the Auschwitz camp.

However, while shooting *Hook*, Spielberg decided he was ready to take on the project. He felt that finally, after years of avoiding it, he had reached a high enough level of personal maturity. One reason he finally changed his mind, he says, was his family: "It was having kids. I got interested for the sake of my children, when they got old enough to ask me questions like, 'Dad, where did you come from? Where did Grandma come from?'"[95]

Finding Schindler

The casting of the film's three main characters was crucial. Amon Goeth, the psychopathic commander of the Nazi camp, and Itzhak Stern, the courageous Jewish accountant who becomes Schindler's right-hand man, were played by a pair of gifted British actors, Ralph Fiennes and Ben Kingsley. Excellent as these actors were, many observers feel that the casting of Schindler himself was truly exceptional.

While in London auditioning actors to play the boy in *Empire*, Spielberg had hired an adult actor to read opposite the young actors. This was an imposing Irishman named Liam Neeson, a struggling actor making ends meet as a housepainter. Spielberg was impressed with Neeson's charisma and deep, distinctive voice, and he told the Irishman they would do something special together someday.

Spielberg encountered Neeson again during preproduction for *Schindler,* when he took Capshaw and her mother to see the actor in a production of Eugene O'Neill's *Anna Christie* on Broadway. Backstage, Mrs. Capshaw remarked how much the play had moved her. Neeson impulsively reached out and hugged her. Later, Kate Capshaw remarked to Spielberg that the gesture was exactly the sort of thing that Schindler would have done.

Although many actors had expressed interest in the role, including Harrison Ford, Mel Gibson, and Daniel Day-Lewis, in the end the part went to Neeson. It was the role of a lifetime, and it would make Neeson an international star.

On Location

Schindler's List was shot in Poland, with an all-Polish crew, in the spring of 1993. Spielberg had hoped to shoot scenes inside the Auschwitz concentration camp, which is now a public memorial. However, Spielberg was denied access by the World Jewish Congress, which feared what it called "Disneyfication" of the Holocaust. The film's Auschwitz scenes were instead shot on a set built adjacent to the real site.

As with *E.T.* and *The Color Purple*, Spielberg did not storyboard. Often, he didn't know how he would shoot a scene until he arrived on the set that day. Most of the film is in black and white, and about 40 percent was shot with a handheld camera.

The result was a rough, documentary-like film unlike anything else Spielberg had ever done. He comments,

> Even with *Empire of the Sun* and *The Color Purple,* my most adult movies to date, those films were done with the same tools I used to make *E.T., Close Encounters,* and

Raiders. I didn't change the toolbox; I simply changed
the project. On this movie I threw out the toolbox and
started from scratch.[96]

Schindler was extremely difficult for Spielberg to make, and he
was in a fragile state for the seventy-odd days of the shoot. He
cried frequently and felt frightened every day, remembering stories of his seventeen family members who had died at the hands
of the Nazis. Fortunately, he had strong support. Capshaw and his
children were there, and his parents and his rabbi visited.

Spielberg Call Home

Spielberg, never strongly religious, experienced a new feeling
toward religion during his stay in Poland. He later said that he was
"hit in the face" with his Jewishness as the memory of his relatives'
stories came rushing back to him. He remarked at the time, "Suddenly I'm flashing back to my childhood and remembering vividly
the stories my parents and grandparents taught me."[97]

Besides dealing with this emotionally draining project,
Spielberg was also juggling a backbreaking schedule on his
other current film. Three nights a week in Poland, he came
home to the small hotel he had rented for his family, switched
on a satellite dish in the front yard, and worked on postproduction for *Jurassic Park.*

Via two satellite channels, one for image and one for voice,
Spielberg could hear the score, oversee the editing, and check
on the computer animation as each of these evolved. Just as
importantly, the satellite link also provided friendly faces and
voices during a difficult emotional time. Spielberg was sometimes so sad in Poland that he would call Robin Williams in California and ask the comic to make him laugh. Williams would
then spend half an hour improvising sketches to cheer up his
faraway friend.

A Surprise Hit

No major studio had ever dealt with the Holocaust so frankly. Furthermore, no one, not even the director, had ever expected a three-
hour film about the most horrifying event of the century to be

Spielberg directs Liam Neeson during the filming of Schindler's List *in Poland. Neeson starred as Oskar Schindler, a Nazi industrialist who saved over eleven hundred Jews from labor camps.*

popular. Spielberg had told Universal executives that they would probably never see a return on their $22 million investment.

He was wrong. When *Schindler's List* was released in December 1993, it was an astonishing surprise hit, grossing $321.2 million worldwide. This unexpected success itself became a major event. It drew public attention to the Holocaust and to ongoing efforts to keep its memory alive. At the same time, the movie drew even stronger reactions than *The Color Purple.*

Many critics were reverently ecstatic over *Schindler. Newsweek's* critic wrote, "This movie will shatter you, but it earns its tears honestly." *The New York Times* commented, "Mr. Spielberg has made sure that neither he nor the Holocaust will ever be thought of in the same way again." And *New York* magazine's critic remarked that it was as if Spielberg "understood for the first time why God gave him such extraordinary skills."[98]

Also, Spielberg was finally acknowledged by the Oscar committee for *Schindler's List.* The movie received eleven nominations and won in seven, including Best Director, Picture, and Adapted Screenplay. Accepting his award, Spielberg said,

I could have dealt with never winning an Academy Award,
because I had practiced dealing with it for the last twelve
years. . . . So this is a wonderful honor tonight. If I hadn't
gotten it, I probably would have been shattered.[99]

Controversy

Some critics and audiences were not impressed, however. They
felt that the movie "Spielbergized" the Holocaust, turning a terrible event and a sacred memory into commercial entertainment. One critic in the *Village Voice* called the movie "a
feel-good entertainment about the ultimate feel-bad experience
of the 20th Century."[100]

Others objected to the emphasis on a Nazi hero, not a Jewish hero. Some thought there was too much attention on living
Jews, too little on those who died. Still others felt there was not
enough focus on individual Jewish figures in the film, with the
exception of Stern.

At the 1994 Academy Awards, Spielberg proudly holds up his two Oscars for Schindler's List.

Still Amusing Themselves

John Baxter, in *Steven Spielberg: The Unauthorized Biography*, comments on how Spielberg's innate optimism persists even amid the horrors of the Holocaust.

However much he fought his impulses, Spielberg couldn't help but make *Schindler's List* an entertainment. . . . His worst characters, even Goeth at his most loathsome, have charm. Nor could Spielberg close his eyes to the persistence of the human spirit. Even in the midst of atrocity, human beings will amuse themselves, do business, fall in love. Krakow Jews improvise a trading exchange in the last place the Nazis will look, the pews of a Catholic church during mass. A wedding is even held in the camp, and a light bulb crushed instead of the traditional glass. These scenes, and another in which men and women huddled round a brazier in the ghetto find time for a few chilly jokes, were to draw accusations that he had "Spielbergised" the Holocaust.

Another objection was that the reasons behind Schindler's change of heart, from Nazi war profiteer to hero, were never made clear. Spielberg's response to this was that the good and bad aspects of a person's character are always present, and that the personality of a complex man like Schindler is always a mystery. In the end, he says, heroism is essentially unexplainable: "I've asked a lot of survivors, both here and in Poland, 'Why do you think Oskar Schindler saved your life?' And most of them say, 'It's not important why he saved my life. It's only important that he did it.'"[101]

Despite the criticisms, *Schindler's List* was overall a tremendous triumph. Together with *Jurassic Park* and Spielberg's entry into a stable marriage, it marked a breakthrough in Spielberg's art and personal life. As the 1990s progressed, he continued to explore his new freedom, alternating roller-coaster spectaculars with more serious-minded films.

Chapter 7

Into the Future

Directing is about seeing twenty moves ahead while you're working on the next five.

—Steven Spielberg

AFTER THE EXHAUSTING experiences of *Jurassic Park* and *Schindler's List,* Spielberg promised his wife that he would take a year off from directing. In fact, it would be three years before he returned to the director's chair.

Spielberg spent most of that time with his family at their home in Pacific Palisades. Although he still read scripts and oversaw productions and business ventures, he was more concerned with spending time with his kids. He recalls, "I was Mr. Carpool. We had breakfast and dinner together every day. It's full-time work, because every one of our kids is a leader. Seven leaders, no followers." [102]

Spielberg had always been close to his mother. Over the years, however, he had remained estranged from his father. Then, as Spielberg settled into being a father himself during his time off, the two reconciled. It succeeded to the point where Spielberg served as best man when Arnold remarried. The director comments:

I didn't want to be so wrapped up in my work as my dad, and yet inexorably [inevitably] I was becoming my dad. So we finally reached out to each other. It was like coming home again, making up for lost time—and we have a lot of lost time between us. Now we're so close, it's fantastic. [103]

Philanthropy

Spielberg has been wealthy for a long time, and his personal net worth has been estimated at nearly $1 billion. For years, he has used some of his money to fund worthy causes.

In 1985, for instance, he gave $100,000 to Harvard for research into extraterrestrial life. A longtime collector of original paintings by Norman Rockwell, he helped underwrite a wing of the Rockwell Museum in Massachusetts. He donated $850,000 for a studio at the Balanchine School of American Ballet and the world premiere of *Jurassic Park* was a fund-raiser for the Children's Defense Fund. The generally apolitical Spielberg has recently made substantial donations to the Democratic Party as well.

The area of philanthropy in which Spielberg has been most generous, however, is Jewish causes. All of his millions in profits for *Schindler's List*, for instance, went to Jewish-related charities such as the Holocaust Museum in Washington, D.C., and the restoration of Anne Frank's house.

During his time off, Spielberg also created the Survivors of the Shoah Visual History Foundation, named for the Hebrew word for "holocaust." This foundation has nearly one hundred full-time staff members in nine offices around the world. They record and preserve the testimony of Holocaust survivors on videotape and other forms of media.

Not Grainy or Tactile

The way film looks to the viewer is crucially different from that of video, as Spielberg points out in this excerpt from Siskel and Ebert's *The Future of the Movies*.

[S]eeing a large image, direct light through the celluloid, projecting like a slide show in movement against a screen with good sound and the smell of popcorn. It's exciting. It's theatrical. It's showmanship. Movies are showmanship. When movies go onto videotape, I love the idea that people still see our films in all different forms, but the showmanship is missing once you look at a movie at home. . . .

A lot of movies in the future will be made high definition, bypassing film and the process of the chemicals in film, and right onto cassette, right into an HDTV receiver. And it's going to look good, I guess, but it's not going to be film. It's not going to be grainy. It's not going to have a tactile vibration to it. Hopefully it's just going to be good storytelling by a different process.

Spielberg and Jeff Goldblum (right), who starred in the movie Jurassic
Park, *light torches to mark the opening of the Jurassic Park ride at
Universal Studios, Hollywood.*

In addition to his philanthropic efforts, Spielberg was active
in other ways during his three years off.

He kept track of a permanent staff of sixty at Amblin. He
also oversaw the switch when longtime colleagues Kathleen
Kennedy and Frank Marshall left to start their own production
company, replacing them with another married couple, Walter
Parkes and Laurie MacDonald. He oversaw several feature productions, including *Twister, The Flintstones,* and *Casper,* as well as
an interactive CD-ROM, "Steven Spielberg's Director's Chair,"
and the Jurassic Park ride at Universal Studios, Hollywood.

During this period and continuing into the present, Spielberg has also invested in several nonfilm projects. These include
a British horse-racing stable, a small software company, a chain
of gourmet submarine sandwich shops that feature a simulated
ride in a genuine sub, and a series of high-tech games arcades
called GameWorks. The first of these, a 30,000-square-foot
installation with 250 arcade games, opened in Seattle in 1997,

and up to 100 more are planned. Writer Ken Neville describes GameWorks as "part virtual-reality center, part video arcade, and part suburban-mall hangout."[104]

DreamWorks SKG

Far and away the biggest venture Spielberg has embarked on, however, is a collaboration that writer Jim Impoco says is "an alliance that could alter the landscape of the entertainment industry."[105]

This is DreamWorks SKG, the first major new studio to start up in Hollywood since 1935. The "Dream Team," as the heads of the new studio were dubbed, are three of the most powerful and influential people in the industry: Spielberg, Jeffrey Katzenberg, and David Geffen.

Katzenberg brought Disney Studios to unprecedented heights of success with such mega-hits as *Aladdin* and *The Lion King*. Geffen's background was as a music-industry powerhouse who had overseen the rise of supergroups like the Eagles through his two labels, Asylum and Geffen Records.

Their venture with Spielberg attracted over $2.5 billion in investment money. Separate departments for film, music, interactive video, and other products were assembled. Deals were signed with a number of highly creative directors and others. Impoco remarks: "One key to success in the movie business is attracting top directors and actors—and it's hard to imagine a more powerful magnet for talent than Spielberg, Geffen and Katzenberg."[106]

A Marathon

Other prominent Hollywood figures had tried similar ventures in the past without success, however. There was considerable speculation within the industry that the new studio might not succeed.

Mocking the widespread feelings of envy within the film community toward the three powerful men, David Letterman joked that now, instead of waiting for the trio to fail separately, Hollywood could wait for them to fail together. Arnold Rifkin, head of the giant William Morris talent agency, added that the pressure to perform was tremendous: "Given who they are, there was a level of expectation far greater than anyone could have achieved." [107]

The studio's early efforts, indeed, were disappointing. Its first movies, an action thriller called *The Peacemaker* and a comedy entitled *MouseHunt*, were lackluster both critically and at the box office. Of the first five TV series the studio produced, only one, *Spin City*, became a hit. Its music division, which relied primarily on established artists like George Michael and Randy Travis, also performed poorly.

However, many industry experts stress that DreamWorks's success or failure cannot be judged by its earliest products. Jack Rapke, who has a production company within DreamWorks, comments, "To look at the initial [output] and draw a conclusion about what this company will really become is a silly exercise." William Savoy, who oversees Microsoft co-founder Paul Allen's half-billion dollar investment in the new studio, adds, "This is a marathon. I'm not concerned. We have three of the best people in the business doing what they're good at." [108]

The Lost World: Jurassic Park

With the exception of the Indy Jones series, Spielberg had never made a sequel. And he had always been disappointed by the sequels that did get made, poor films over which he had no control. Kathleen Kennedy remarks, "Steven still harbors a bit of regret about the way *Jaws II* and *III* turned out." [109]

Spielberg had never made a sequel because he had been uninterested in continuing the story. What convinced him to take on a sequel to *Jurassic Park*, when he finally took up directing again, was a compelling story by Michael Crichton and screenwriter David Koepp. Spielberg remarks, "If I hadn't found a [second] story I was interested in, *Jurassic Park* would have remained just a nice memory for me." [110]

The Lost World: Jurassic Park postulated that a few dinosaurs survived from the park. A scientist who is studying them is also the girlfriend of Ian Malcolm, the mathematician returning from the first film. When things go wrong, they are thrown into a desperate struggle to survive. At the same time, an unscrupulous businessman is secretly bringing a dinosaur from the island to a second park in San Diego, California.

The section of the film in which San Diego was attacked was a tribute to the classic Japanese monster movies of the 1950s, in which giant creatures destroy city after city. Spielberg took the opportunity to have fun. Among those fleeing the dinosaur in *The Lost World*, for instance, is a Japanese businessman who screams, in Japanese, "I left Tokyo to get away from this!" As Spielberg watched playbacks of this and other scenes, he happily said, "I've waited my whole life to do a Godzilla movie."[111]

Once again, *The Lost World*'s dinosaurs, although on screen for only a few minutes, were the focus of attention. They were created, as in the first film, with a combination of computer graphics and animatronic models. The difference was that the technology and knowledge for creating them had advanced tremendously since *Jurassic Park*. Animation director Phil Tippett compared the experience to a priceless violin: "We built the Stradivarius, now we're learning to play it."[112]

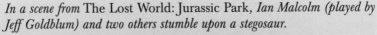

In a scene from The Lost World: Jurassic Park, *Ian Malcolm (played by Jeff Goldblum) and two others stumble upon a stegosaur.*

Amistad

The success of *The Lost World* was almost inevitable; it earned a massive $229 million worldwide after its release in May 1997. This success was based on its essential nature as a "popcorn movie"—a fantastic premise, non-stop thrills, and unparalleled special effects. Spielberg followed it in December 1997 with a very different film: *Amistad,* a serious historical drama, based on a true incident, that explores controversial issues of race, politics, and human rights.

Amistad told the story of slaves being transported to the Caribbean in 1839. They revolted, killed the crew of the ship, and tried to return to Africa. They were captured off America and put on trial for murder. Their case was argued before the U.S. Supreme Court by former president John Quincy Adams.

Reviews and box-office receipts for *Amistad* were respectable but not overwhelming. In general, critics were far less enthusiastic than they had been about Spielberg's previous drama, *Schindler's List.* Leah Rozen's reaction in *People Weekly* was typical: "The movie seems more dutiful than dramatic; with [a few exceptions] it lacks the well-drawn, complex central characters who made . . . *Schindler's List* a masterpiece.[113]

Amistad was the center of controversy just before its opening due to a lawsuit filed by novelist Barbara Chase-Riboud. The writer argued that Spielberg and his screenwriters, Steve Zaillian and David Franzoni, plagiarized her 1989 novel *Echo of Lions.* However, the courts ruled that Chase-Riboud's case lacked sufficient merit. *Time* critic Richard Schickel commented, "It's a shame that *Amistad*'s release has been polluted with charges of plagiarism, for what's on the screen has an emotional and moral weight that is entirely its own."[114]

Into the Future

Spielberg's next directorial effort, released in June 1998, was also an intimate drama set against a larger backdrop. *Saving Private Ryan,* starring Tom Hanks and Matt Damon, concerned the search for a single soldier during the decisive D-day invasion of World War II.

As Spielberg moves into his fifth decade, his life revolves around balance: balancing action films (including a planned fourth Indy Jones movie) with more serious projects, balancing life on the west and east coasts, balancing family and work.

This balance requires juggling several domains. Spielberg is, first of all, a gifted artist. At the same time, he is the most commercially successful filmmaker in history; in 1997 *Forbes* magazine placed him at the top of its list of entertainers. (In second place was George Lucas, and third and fourth places were held by two more old friends: Oprah Winfrey and Michael Crichton.)

As he approached middle age, Spielberg was also able to find a relatively stable home life, a close-knit family, and long-time, trusted work colleagues. This atmosphere has allowed the director to put to rest some of the fear, self-doubt, loneliness, and compulsive work habits that plagued him earlier in his life. And yet he appears to retain much of the boyish enthusiasm for life that marked his earlier days.

The environment that Spielberg has surrounded himself with, in many ways, mirrors the basic message of virtually all his movies: a positive, optimistic vision of life. Film historian Douglas Brode points out that "in addition to remarkable talents for providing entertainment, he more importantly reassures his audience, again and again, that there is hope."[115]

Steven Spielberg appears to have found a measure of balance in his personal life as well as in his art. Movie fans around the world hope that it will, in the future, continue to inspire his fertile imagination.

Notes

Introduction: Hollywood Icon

1. Quoted in Richard Corliss and Jeffrey Ressner, "Peter Pan Grows Up: But Can He Still Fly?" *Time,* May 19, 1997.
2. Quoted in Donald R. Mott and Cheryl McAllister Saunders, *Steven Spielberg.* Boston: Twayne Publishers, 1986, p. 12.
3. Quoted in Frank Sanello, *Spielberg: The Man, the Movies, the Mythology.* Dallas, TX: Taylor Publishing, 1996, p. 197.
4. Quoted in Martin Amis, *The Moronic Inferno.* Harmondsworth, England: Viking Penguin, 1987, p. 154.
5. Quoted in Corliss and Ressner, "Peter Pan Grows Up."
6. Quoted in Stephen Farber and Marc Green, *Outrageous Conduct: Art, Ego, and the "Twilight Zone" Case.* New York: Morrow, 1988, p. 43.
7. Amis, *The Moronic Inferno,* p. 147.
8. Quoted in John Baxter, *Steven Spielberg: The Unauthorized Biography.* New York: HarperCollins, 1996, p. 26.
9. Quoted in Roger Ebert and Gene Siskel, *The Future of the Movies.* Kansas City: Andrews & McMeel, 1991, p. 39.

Chapter 1: A Formative Childhood

10. Quoted in Baxter, *Steven Spielberg: The Unauthorized Biography,* p. 19.
11. Quoted in Sanello, *Spielberg: The Man, the Movies, the Mythology,* p. 13.
12. Quoted in Mott and Saunders, *Steven Spielberg,* p. 12.
13. Quoted in Philip M. Taylor, *Steven Spielberg: The Man, His Movies and Their Meaning.* New York: Continuum, 1994, p. 52.
14. Quoted in Amis, *The Moronic Inferno,* p. 149.

15. Quoted in Joseph McBride, *Steven Spielberg: A Biography*. New York: Simon & Schuster, 1997, p.47.

Chapter 2: Early Films, Early Themes

16. Quoted in McBride, *Steven Spielberg: A Biography*, p. 67.
17. Quoted in Amis, *The Moronic Inferno*, p. 149.
18. Quoted in Sanello, *Spielberg: The Man, the Movies, the Mythology*, p. 14.
19. Quoted in McBride, *Steven Spielberg: A Biography*, p. 12.
20. Quoted in McBride, *Steven Spielberg: A Biography*, pp. 12–13.
21. Quoted in Baxter, *Steven Spielberg: The Unauthorized Biography*, p. 36.
22. Quoted in Amis, *The Moronic Inferno*, p. 148.
23. Quoted in McBride, *Steven Spielberg: A Biography*, p. 12.
24. Quoted in McBride, *Steven Spielberg: A Biography*, p. 90.
25. Quoted in McBride, *Steven Spielberg: A Biography*, p. 101.
26. Quoted in Sanello, *Spielberg: The Man, the Movies, the Mythology*, p. 22.

Chapter 3: Self-Education and Professional Breakthroughs

27. Michael Pye and Lynda Myles, *The Movie Brats: How the Film Generation Took Over Hollywood*. New York: Holt, Rinehart & Winston, 1979, p. 222.
28. Quoted in Douglas Brode, *The Films of Steven Spielberg*. New York: Citadel Press, 1995, p. 17.
29. Quoted in McBride, *Steven Spielberg: A Biography*, p. 138.
30. Quoted in Sanello, *Spielberg: The Man, the Movies, the Mythology*, p. 27.
31. Quoted in Baxter, *Steven Spielberg: The Unauthorized Biography*, p. 53.
32. Quoted in Sanello, *Spielberg: The Man, the Movies, the Mythology*, p. 30.
33. Quoted in Farber and Green, *Outrageous Conduct*, p. 63.
34. Quoted in McBride, *Steven Spielberg: A Biography*, p. 176.
35. Quoted in Farber and Green, *Outrageous Conduct*, p.42.
36. Mott and Saunders, *Steven Spielberg*, p. 19.
37. Quoted in Pye and Myles, *The Movie Brats*, pp. 223–24.
38. Quoted in Mott and Saunders, *Steven Spielberg*, p. 19.
39. Pye and Myles, *The Movie Brats*, p. 231.

40. Quoted in McBride, *Steven Spielberg: A Biography*, p. 215.
41. Quoted in Baxter, *Steven Spielberg: The Unauthorized Biography*, p. 107.
42. Quoted in Taylor, *Steven Spielberg: The Man, His Movies and Their Meaning*, p. 50.
43. Quoted in McBride, *Steven Spielberg: A Biography*, pp. 223–24.

Chapter 4: The Blockbuster Years

44. Baxter, *Steven Spielberg: The Unauthorized Biography*, p. 108.
45. Pye and Myles, *The Movie Brats*, p. 232.
46. Quoted in McBride, *Steven Spielberg: A Biography*, p. 260.
47. Quoted in Taylor, *Steven Spielberg: The Man, His Movies and Their Meaning*, p. 92.
48. Quoted in Mott and Saunders, *Steven Spielberg*, p. 57.
49. Quoted in Mott and Saunders, *Steven Spielberg*, p. 76.
50. Quoted in Brode, *The Films of Steven Spielberg*, p. 86.
51. Quoted in Sanello, *Spielberg: The Man, the Movies, the Mythology*, p. 101.
52. Quoted in Amis, *The Moronic Inferno*, p. 151.
53. Quoted in Brode, *The Films of Steven Spielberg*, p. 90.
54. Quoted in Julia Phillips, *You'll Never Eat Lunch in This Town Again*. New York: Random House, 1991, p. 264.
55. Quoted in Baxter, *Steven Spielberg: The Unauthorized Biography*, p. 200.
56. Quoted in McBride, *Steven Spielberg: A Biography*, p. 318.
57. Quoted in Amis, *The Moronic Inferno*, p. 152.
58. Quoted in Taylor, *Steven Spielberg: The Man, His Movies and Their Meaning*, p. 14.
59. Quoted in McBride, *Steven Spielberg: A Biography*, p. 333.
60. Amis, *The Moronic Inferno*, p. 147.
61. Quoted in Baxter, *Steven Spielberg: The Unauthorized Biography*, p. 238.
62. Quoted in Farber and Green, *Outrageous Conduct*, p. 158.
63. Quoted in Taylor, *Steven Spielberg: The Man, His Movies and Their Meaning*, p. 110.
64. Quoted in Ron LaBrecque, *Special Effects: Disaster at "Twilight Zone"—The Tragedy and the Trial*. New York: Scribner's, 1988, p. 129.
65. Farber and Green, *Outrageous Conduct*, p. 46.

Chapter 5: New Directions, New Family

66. Amis, *The Moronic Inferno*, p. 150.
67. Quoted in LaBrecque, *Special Effects*, p. 127.
68. Quoted in McBride, *Steven Spielberg: A Biography*, p. 365.
69. Quoted in Taylor, *Steven Spielberg: The Man, His Movies and Their Meaning*, p. 113.
70. Quoted in Taylor, *Steven Spielberg: The Man, His Movies and Their Meaning*, p. 113.
71. Quoted in McBride, *Steven Spielberg: A Biography*, p. 371.
72. Quoted in McBride, *Steven Spielberg: A Biography*, p. 373.
73. Quoted in McBride, *Steven Spielberg: A Biography*, p. 373.
74. Quoted in Taylor, *Steven Spielberg: The Man, His Movies and Their Meaning*, p. 118.
75. Quoted in McBride, *Steven Spielberg: A Biography*, p. 377.
76. Quoted in Brode, *The Films of Steven Spielberg*, p. 23.
77. Quoted in McBride, *Steven Spielberg: A Biography*, p. 382.
78. Quoted in Brode, *The Films of Steven Spielberg*, p. 162.
79 Quoted in McBride, *Steven Spielberg: A Biography*, p. 398.
80. Quoted in Sanello, *Spielberg: The Man, the Movies, the Mythology*, p. 184.
81. Quoted in McBride, *Steven Spielberg: A Biography*, p. 401.
82. Quoted in McBride, *Steven Spielberg: A Biography*, p. 402.
83. Quoted in Brode, *The Films of Steven Spielberg*, p. 197.
84. Quoted in Baxter, *Steven Spielberg: The Unauthorized Biography*, pp. 330–31.
85. Quoted in Ebert and Siskel, *The Future of the Movies*, p. 52.
86. Quoted in Taylor, *Steven Spielberg: The Man, His Movies and Their Meaning*, p. 148.
87. Quoted in Baxter, *Steven Spielberg: The Unauthorized Biography*, p. 367.
88. Quoted in Brode, *The Films of Steven Spielberg*, p. 120.
89. Quoted in Taylor, *Steven Spielberg: The Man, His Movies and Their Meaning*, p. 123.

Chapter 6: Maturity at Home and on the Screen

90. Quoted in Julie Salamon, "The Long Voyage Home," *Harper's Bazaar*, February 1994.
91. Quoted in David Ansen, "Spielberg's Obsession," *Newsweek*, December 20, 1993.
92. Brode, *The Films of Steven Spielberg*, p. 222.

93. Jody Duncan, *The Making of The Lost World: Jurassic Park.* New York: Ballantine Books, 1997, p. 1.
94. David Thomson, "Presenting Enamelware," *Film Comment,* March/April 1994.
95. Quoted in Salamon, "The Long Voyage Home."
96. Quoted in Salamon, "The Long Voyage Home."
97. Quoted in Salamon, "The Long Voyage Home."
98. Quoted in McBride, *Steven Spielberg: A Biography,* p. 434.
99. Quoted in McBride, *Steven Spielberg: A Biography,* p. 436.
100. Quoted in Brode, *The Films of Steven Spielberg,* p. 240.
101. Quoted in Edward Guthmann, "Spielberg's 'List': Director Rediscovers His Jewishness While Filming Nazi Story," *San Francisco Chronicle,* December 12, 1993.

Chapter 7: Into the Future

102. Quoted in Corliss and Ressner, "Peter Pan Grows Up."
103. Quoted in Corliss and Ressner, "Peter Pan Grows Up."
104. Ken Neville, "Playing for Keeps," *Entertainment Weekly,* April 25, 1997.
105. Jim Impoco, "Hollywood's Dream Team: Talented Trio Forms a New Entertainment Company to Vie with the Studios," *U.S. News & World Report,* October 24, 1994.
106. Impoco, "Hollywood's Dream Team."
107. Quoted in Josh Young, "Needs Improvement," *Entertainment Weekly,* October 17, 1997.
108. Quoted in Josh Young, "Needs Improvement."
109 Quoted in Corliss and Ressner, "Peter Pan Grows Up."
110. Quoted in Duncan, *The Making of The Lost World,* p. 158.
111. Quoted in Duncan, *The Making of The Lost World,* p. 119.
112. Quoted in Duncan, *The Making of The Lost World,* p. 15.
113. Leah Rozen, "Amistad," *People Weekly,* December 15, 1997.
114. Richard Schickel, "Amistad," *Time,* December 15, 1997.
115. Brode, *The Films of Steven Spielberg,* p. 241.

Important Dates in the Life of Steven Spielberg

1946
Steven Spielberg is born in Cincinnati, Ohio, on December 18.
1957
Moves with family to Scottsdale, a suburb of Phoenix, Arizona.
1958
Begins making home movies with father's 8-millimeter camera.
1964
First full-length film, *Firelight,* premieres at local movie theater; moves with family to Saratoga, California.
1967–1969
Attends California State University at Long Beach and has an informal apprenticeship at Universal Studios.
1968
Produces and directs short film, *Amblin',* that is well-received by Universal executives; receives contract to direct for Universal Studios television department.
1969
Directs first show for TV, an episode of *Night Gallery.*
1971
First full-length TV film, *Duel,* premieres.
1974
First theatrical feature, *The Sugarland Express,* is released.
1975
Jaws is released.

1977
Close Encounters of the Third Kind is released.
1979
1941 is released.
1980
Close Encounters of the Third Kind: The Special Edition is released.
1981
Raiders of the Lost Ark is released.
1982
E.T.: The Extra-Terrestrial and *Poltergeist* are released.
1983
Twilight Zone—The Movie is released; Amblin' (later Amblin) Entertainment offices are established.
1984
Indiana Jones and the Temple of Doom is released.
1985
Marries Amy Irving; *The Color Purple* is released.
1987
Empire of the Sun is released.
1989
Divorces Amy Irving; *Indiana Jones and the Last Crusade* and *Always* are released.
1991
Marries Kate Capshaw; *Hook* is released.
1993
Jurassic Park and *Schindler's List* are released.
1994
Receives Best Director Oscar for *Schindler's List;* establishes Survivors of the Shoah foundation; co-founds DreamWorks SKG, a major multimedia studio.
1997
The Lost World: Jurassic Park and *Amistad* are released.
1998
Saving Private Ryan is released.

Filmography

Feature films directed by Steven Spielberg

Duel (made for TV, 1971)

Something Evil (made for TV, 1972)

Savage (made for TV, 1972)

The Sugarland Express (1974)

Jaws (1975)

Close Encounters of the Third Kind (1977)

1941 (1979)

Close Encounters of the Third Kind: The Special Edition (1980)

Raiders of the Lost Ark (1981)

E.T.: The Extra-Terrestrial (1982)

Twilight Zone—The Movie ("Kick the Can" segment) (1983)

Indiana Jones and the Temple of Doom (1984)

The Color Purple (1985)

Empire of the Sun (1987)

Indiana Jones and the Last Crusade (1989)

Always (1989)

Hook (1991)

Jurassic Park (1993)

Schindler's List (1993)

The Lost World: Jurassic Park (1997)

Amistad (1997)

Saving Private Ryan (1998)

For Further Reading

Tom Collins, *Steven Spielberg: Creator of E.T.* Minneapolis, MN: Dillon Press, 1983. This basic and somewhat dated book for young children focuses on the plots of Spielberg's movies as well as his life. Lists Spielberg's birth year incorrectly as 1947, a common mistake as until recently the filmmaker gave that year to interviewers as his birth year.

Thomas Conklin, *Meet Steven Spielberg.* New York: Random House, 1994. A brief paperback biography, this book lacks footnotes and index.

Jody Duncan, *The Making of The Lost World: Jurassic Park.* New York: Ballantine Books, 1997. A large and heavily illustrated peek behind the scenes of one of Spielberg's effects-heavy works, written by the editor of *Cinefex* magazine. Not written specifically for young adults, but very readable.

Elizabeth Ferber, *Steven Spielberg.* Philadelphia: Chelsea House, 1997. This look at Spielberg's life and career up to *Schindler's List* is well written but has no footnotes or attributions.

Jim Hargrove, *Steven Spielberg: Amazing Filmmaker.* Chicago: Childrens Press, 1988. A good introduction for young adults, though outdated.

D. M. Mabery, *Steven Spielberg.* Minneapolis, MN: Lerner Publications, 1987. This brief book for younger children is out-of-date now.

Virginia Meachum, *Steven Spielberg: Hollywood Filmmaker.* Springfield, NJ: Enslow Publishers, 1996. A well-written introduction to Spielberg's life with a good filmography.

Tom Powers, *Steven Spielberg: Master Storyteller.* Minneapolis, MN: Lerner Publications, 1997. This book about Spielberg's life has some useful documentation in its footnotes.

Works Consulted

Books

Martin Amis, *The Moronic Inferno*. Harmondsworth, England: Viking Penguin, 1987. (Paperback edition of a book published originally in 1986). This perceptive collection of essays on American culture by a leading British writer includes "Steven Spielberg: Boyish Wonder."

John Baxter, *Steven Spielberg: The Unauthorized Biography*. New York: HarperCollins, 1996. The usefulness of this work, by a British film critic, is marred by occasional mean-spiritedness and the inclusion of too much gossipy information.

Douglas Brode, *The Films of Steven Spielberg*. New York: Citadel Press, 1995. This is a useful, in-depth resource by a perceptive film critic, though it is quite technical at times.

Roger Ebert and Gene Siskel, *The Future of the Movies*. Kansas City: Andrews & McMeel, 1991. Fascinating and insightful interviews, by the well-known film critics, with some of the best-known "movie brats," including Spielberg.

Stephen Farber and Marc Green, *Outrageous Conduct: Art, Ego, and the "Twilight Zone" Case*. New York: Morrow, 1988. This account of the *Twilight Zone* tragedy is heavily biased; Farber has long been a harsh critic of Spielberg's films.

Ron LaBrecque, *Special Effects: Disaster at "Twilight Zone"—Tragedy and the Trial*. New York: Scribner's, 1988. A respected investigative journalist takes an evenhanded look at the *Twilight Zone* affair.

Joseph McBride, *Steven Spielberg: A Biography*. New York: Simon & Schuster, 1997. An excellent book by a well-respected biographer of film directors; thoroughly researched, clearly written, and copiously footnoted, this is the best single biography of Spielberg to date.

Donald R. Mott and Cheryl McAllister Saunders, *Steven Spielberg*. Boston: Twayne Publishers, 1986. An early look at Spielberg's work by a pair of film critics, focusing mainly on technical analyses.

Julia Phillips, *You'll Never Eat Lunch in This Town Again*. New York: Random House, 1991. This raunchy kiss-and-tell book, by the troubled coproducer of *Close Encounters,* is largely about her own problems with cocaine abuse, but it does have some sections about Spielberg.

Michael Pye and Lynda Myles, *The Movie Brats: How the Film Generation Took Over Hollywood*. New York: Holt, Rinehart & Winston, 1979. Two British journalists look at an influential generation of film directors, including Scorsese, Milius, Coppola, Lucas, and Spielberg.

Frank Sanello, *Spielberg: The Man, the Movies, the Mythology*. Dallas, TX: Taylor Publishing, 1996. A perfunctory effort by a show-business writer, but written in a simple style that makes generous use of quotations from newspaper and magazine articles.

Philip M. Taylor, *Steven Spielberg: The Man, His Movies and Their Meaning*. New York: Continuum, 1994. A British professor of communications and film expert focuses on the meanings of Spielberg's movies in society and film history.

Periodicals

David Ansen, "Spielberg's Obsession," *Newsweek,* December 20, 1993. A lengthy article about *Schindler's List.*

Richard Corliss and Jeffrey Ressner, "Peter Pan Grows Up: But Can He Still Fly?" *Time,* May 19, 1997. A lengthy profile and interview of Spielberg, focusing on his projects following his three-year sabbatical after completing *Schindler's List.*

Edward Guthmann, "Spielberg's 'List': Director Rediscovers His Jewishness While Filming Nazi Story," *San Francisco Chronicle,* December 12, 1993. A piece on the effect of *Schindler's List* on the director.

Jim Impoco, "Hollywood's Dream Team: Talented Trio Forms a New Entertainment Company to Vie with the Studios," *U.S.*

News & World Report, October 24, 1994. Announces the formation of DreamWorks SKG.

Ken Neville, "Playing for Keeps," *Entertainment Weekly,* April 25, 1997. A brief article on the GameWorks adult arcade.

Dale Pollock, "Spielberg Philosophical over ET Oscar Defeat," *Los Angeles Times,* April 13, 1983. An interview in which, among other things, Spielberg breaks his silence over the *Twilight Zone* tragedy.

Leah Rozen, "Amistad," *People Weekly,* December 15, 1997. A review of the movie.

Julie Salamon, "The Long Voyage Home," *Harper's Bazaar,* February 1994. A lengthy profile of Spielberg and his family at home.

Paul M. Sammon, "Turn On Your Heartlight: Inside *E.T.*" *Cinefex,* January 1983. An illustrated article on the special effects of *E.T.*

Richard Schickel, "Amistad," *Time,* December 15, 1997. A review of the movie.

David Thomson, "Presenting Enamelware," *Film Comment,* March/April 1994. A critique of *Schindler's List* and *Jurassic Park.*

Josh Young, "Needs Improvement," *Entertainment Weekly,* October 17, 1997. About the disappointing first productions of DreamWorks's movie division.

Index

Picture Credits

Cover photo: Photofest
AP Photo/Chris Pizzello, 17, 25
AP Photo/ho-Premier, 48
AP/Wide World, 8, 45
Archive Photos, 50, 90
Archive Photos/Darlene Hammond, 37
Archive Photos/Fotos International, 55 (bottom)
Archive Photos/Fotos International/Frank Edwards, 14
Columbia Pictures/Archive Photos, 22
Handout/Reuters/Archive Photos, 93
Photofest, 10, 11, 18, 27, 30, 39 (both), 42, 44, 49, 52, 55 (top),
    57, 59, 64, 65, 67, 70, 72, 74, 79, 81, 85, 94
Reuters/Blake Sell, Archive Photos, 35
Reuters/Corbis-Bettmann, 9, 86
Reuters/Fred Prouser/Archive Photos, 96
Reuters/Rose Prouser/Archive Photos, 77
John Springer/Corbis-Bettmann, 31

About the Author

Adam Woog has written over a dozen books for adults and younger readers. He lives in his hometown of Seattle, Washington, with his wife and young daughter. Like Steven Spielberg, he is a descendant of European Jewish immigrants.